Monk's Travels

✦

People, Places, and Events

Also by Reverend Edward A. Malloy, C.S.C.

*Monk's Reflections:
A View from the Dome*

Monk's Travels

People, Places, and Events

REVEREND EDWARD A. MALLOY, C.S.C.

**Andrews McMeel
Publishing**

Kansas City

04 05 06 07 08 FFG 10 9 8 7 6 5 4 3 2 1

Library of Congress Cataloging-in-Publication Data

Malloy, Edward A.
   Monk's travels : people, places, and events / Edward A. Malloy.
      p. cm.
   ISBN 0-7407-4706-1
   1. Malloy, Edward A.–Travel. 2. University of Notre Dame–
Presidents–Travel. 3. Voyages and travels. I. Title.

G465.M363 2004
910.4'1–dc22

                                                      2004047733

*I dedicate this book to my sisters,
Mary Long and Joanne Rorapaugh,
in appreciation of their love and
support through the years.*

CONTENTS

LATIN AMERICA

SOUTH AMERICA

AFRICA

DOWN UNDER

THE FAR EAST

SNAPSHOTS

Monk's Travels

❖

People, Places, and Events

PREFACE

This book has its roots in experiences I participated in as an undergraduate student. Between my junior year of college and the end of my first year of seminary, I participated in three successive summer service projects in Latin America. On the first trip to Aguascalientes, Mexico, I was asked by my fellow volunteers to keep a diary of our trip so that we could submit a report to the benefactors who had helped make it possible. I found that keeping a diary not only served that pragmatic purpose but also helped me to focus on the events that were most significant and influential. It also provided a handy reprise of the trip as a whole. On my second and third trips to Peru and Mexico, I also kept a diary, and I discovered that many members of my family and extended friendship group enjoyed sharing vicariously in the experience when I sent a copy of my diary to them.

Many years later, when I first began traveling abroad as President of Notre Dame, I decided to take the same tack. My initial audience was intended to be the members of my family, close personal friends, and fellow members of the University administration. However, I found rather quickly that other people, when they learned about the diary, expressed a desire to have access to its contents. As a result, much more quickly than I had originally imagined, the circle of those who were recipients of my diaries expanded quite broadly. It began to include the members of the University Board of Trustees, Advisory Council members, members of the Alumni Board and past Alumni presidents, and some of the major benefactors as well.

As time went on, I began to modify the contents somewhat by including an early summary of my personal activities since the last diary. This was intended partially as material for the Archives as well as a kind of quick summary of major events on and off the campus that had taken place in this country.

Right from the start, my intention had more to do with capturing the spirit of daily events on my international trips than with providing a finely honed, stylized document. My diaries were never intended to be literary documents or to call for a rewriting after the fact. My style of composition was generally at the end of each day to spend some time writing in hand the major events and persons that I had encountered during the day. Some trips turned out to be more exciting than others. Some of the places that I visited were strange and exotic, and others were more familiar.

On the vast majority of my international trips, I have been in the company of one or more members of the University administration and/or their spouses. In that sense, the prism through which I have interpreted things included regular conversations with my fellow travelers, with whom I also shared experiences of prayer, meals, and entertainment. On none of my trips did I go primarily as a tourist, but there have been good opportunities to simply see the land, enjoy the culture, and appreciate the diversity of the world's population.

A quick summary of the constituencies that were often visited would include Notre Dame graduates, representatives of various church communities, other higher education institutions and systems of education, government leaders, and members of the business and civic communities. I have had the good fortune to visit with many heads of state and cabinet-level officers as well as Catholic Church leaders and representatives of other faith traditions. But I also spent a good amount of time with ordinary folk who helped interpret the culture and/or provided an entree to situations that I would otherwise never have had access to.

Overall, I have been blessed with good health on my trips, but I had a few setbacks along the way as well: altitude sickness in Peru and Tibet; intestinal disorders in Mexico, Chile, and a few other Latin American countries; and temporary rumblings from strange food in various places in Asia and in Africa. These periods of unpleasantness were far outweighed by the stimulating and enjoyable times that have given me a much broader horizon of experience and that I continue to draw on in my professional responsibilities.

Ann Tyler wrote a novel entitled *The Accidental Tourist* that is about a man who is forced to travel but does not want to have any new experiences. He wants to guarantee his safety and security by making sure that everything is predictable and familiar. My goal on my trips was just the opposite: not to do anything too foolish, but to be open to an endless round of new experiences and possibilities. Along the way I have flown in every kind of airplane and in helicopters, been on various kinds of ships and boats, traveled by car, bus, and train, and even boarded an occasional camel or horse (if only to have a dramatic picture taken). I have been stopped by police but never arrested. I have been in semi-dangerous situations but never personally harmed.

One tradition of our traveling groups was to celebrate daily Mass together no matter where we might be. I have taken special pleasure in celebrating Mass in a number of Communist countries or countries recently freed from Soviet control. Among the Masses I have participated in, none were more memorable than the times that I concelebrated with Pope John Paul II in his private chapel at the Vatican.

In the course of my travels, I visited many of the best universities of the world, and some neophyte institutions as well. It is relatively easy for a university person to feel comfortable in another higher education institution. We share a general mission and often have the same kinds of problems. The leaders of these institutions have been invariably generous and kind as they provided tours of their schools or gathered us together for special convocations or other types of meetings. Obviously, I felt a special affinity for the Catholic universities that I visited. They are one concrete manifestation of the "small 'c'" notion of the Catholic Church, that is, as a universal presence of Christ the Teacher and Christ the Light.

The present manuscript represents only a small portion of the diaries that I have offered through the years.

It gathers together material that I believe might be of special interest to a broader audience. In the last part of the book I have included a series of snapshots of interesting people I have met along the way. I chose them because of their name recognition and/or their status and influence in either the world or their national communities.

I have had many trusted companions on my various journeys, including a number of my administrative colleagues here at Notre Dame. These include Tim and Jean O'Meara; Frank and Mary Castellino; Bill and Ann Sexton; Nathan and Julie Hatch; Jim McDonald, C.S.C.; Dave Morrissey; Lou Nanni; Matt Cullinan; Mark Poorman, C.S.C.; Tim Scully, C.S.C.; Dick Warner, C.S.C.; Roberto Gutiérrez; Chandra Johnson; John Affleck-Graves; Roland Smith; Bill Beauchamp, C.S.C.; Bill Seetch, C.S.C.; and many others who were part of the travel parties on some of my trips.

I offer a special word of appreciation to Walt Collins, who has helped me in every stage of the production of this book. As longtime and former editor of *Notre Dame* magazine, he knows the University community well and has helped me decide what should be included and what should be put aside.

JOURNEY THROUGH 9/11 AND BEYOND

During three trips to Europe in the summer of 2001, I visited ten countries and many capital cities. Everywhere I found a sense of relaxation and festivity. The public parks were filled, the airports were crowded, and the harbors were abuzz with activity. Thousands and thousands of Americans were on tour, and while there was some concern about a downturn in the economy, it was viewed from the vantage point of the longest period of economic growth in our history. Assuredly, there were troubling events in many parts of the world, including a complete breakdown in the Middle East peace process, periodic terrorist attacks in Sri Lanka, further unraveling of the former Yugoslavia, Christian–Muslim riots, killings in Indonesia, Nigeria, and other parts of Africa, attacks on Russian forces in Chechnya, and saber rattling by China over Taiwan. Despite all that, most Americans carried a generalized sense of assurance about their place in the world and about the future, in the aftermath of the disputed presidential elections in 2000.

Then came September 11.

I was in my room in Sorin Hall that morning when I received a telephone call from my secretary, Joan Bradley. "Turn on the television," she said. Like most Americans,

I watched the horror unfold. I had scheduled a meeting at 9:30 A.M. for the people who report directly to me, and in light of what was taking place I expanded the invitation to all available members of the University Officers' Group, plus several others who I thought would have a special role to play in the coming days. We made a collective decision to call off classes and declare a day of prayer and reflection. We then tried to decide what fundamental tasks needed to be attended to that day.

First, we wanted to be in touch with the faculty, the staff, and especially the rectors and head staffs in the dorms. Once the word got out that classes had been called off, we wanted to have convenient and comfortable places for students to bring their cares and concerns, and we decided that the dorms would be the best focal points. We also wanted to mobilize the staffs of the University Counseling Center and the Campus Ministry, and as many faculty as we could reach with voice mail and Internet communications.

Second, we wanted to make every effort to give our Muslim students, and others who came from international backgrounds, a sense that they were an integral part of our family and that we would do everything we could to attend to their needs in the coming days. We wanted to make sure, in all our public pronouncements, that we separated out the evil deeds of the terrorists from the orthodox teachings of Islam.

Third, we wanted to be sure that our international-program centers were in communication with the campus and that they were provided with special instructions to guide the students entrusted to them about how to act and dress in light of the events.

Finally, we wanted to secure the very best information available to keep track of the impact of the terrorist acts on members of the Notre Dame family. Through an early computer check, we discovered that at least fifty parents worked in the World Trade Center, and I knew from many visits to New York City that we had many alumni who worked in those facilities as well. We also knew that we could have had some loss of life at the Pentagon and in any of the four planes that crashed. The Alumni Association was particularly helpful in gathering information and making it available to the broader Notre Dame family.

We decided to schedule a Mass of Remembrance, to which we would invite the whole Notre Dame community. Because it was a warm and sunny day, we chose the South Quadrangle for the Mass. After lunch, I took a long and slow walk around Saint Mary's Lake, and I remember with great vividness the sense of serenity that prevailed on campus. The ducks were sleeping, there was almost no noise, and in the distance I could hear the tolling of the funeral bell in Sacred Heart Basilica. It seemed such a contrast between that scene and the ones I had witnessed on television during the course of the day.

On the South Quad, our police and fire department members were present in double numbers to prepare for whatever might happen during the Mass. An ambulance was parked at the circle, and about three hundred choir members from various Notre Dame liturgical choir groups were rehearsing. At 2:15 I glanced at the flag standing at half-staff and wondered what kind of a turnout we might have. Around 2:40 I walked to the Knights of Columbus building, where the concelebrants were assembling. Right at 3:00 we began our procession to the stage, and when I looked out over the assembled group of almost ten thousand faculty, staff, students, and townspeople, I was simply awestruck at the collective witness.

I began the Mass with some general reflections, inviting everyone present to remember those who had lost their lives, and the family members who were mourning or anxious to hear whether their loved ones were still alive. In my homily I spoke of the reality of evil, the sense of tragic loss, the uncertainty about the future, and our need for one another and for the living God. I invoked the image suggested by the beautiful text right below the statue of the Sacred Heart in front of the Main Building. It says *Venite ad me Omnes:* "Come To Me All You Who Are Weary And Heavy Burdened And I Will Give You Rest, For My Yoke Is Easy And My Burden Light." I also spoke of our responsibility to make sure that every member of our family felt protected and included, and that we avoid any scapegoating or misplaced anger directed at parts of the world population. Finally, I called for continued prayers for peace and for the safety of those who were conducting the rescue efforts.

At the Lord's Prayer the majority of students, instead of holding hands as they usually do, locked arms the way they do when we sing the Alma Mater at events. This provided a great sense of intimacy and mutual support in the context of the liturgy. It took quite a bit of time for the fifty concelebrants to distribute Communion, but everybody was patient and indeed seemed to welcome that quiet time for reflection and prayer.

At the end of Mass, I mentioned that Student Government was putting together a blood drive, and I encouraged the members of our community to participate. When Mass was over, everyone stood in silence as we processed down from the stage and walked through the crowd back to the Knights of Columbus building. I had a sense that no one really wanted to leave, that there was something comforting about being together at this challenging moment. In all my time at Notre Dame, I can think of no event more memorable for me than this one. It symbolized all that is best about Notre Dame.

In the following days, many other things had to be taken care of. All the schools in the Big East Conference decided to cancel the weekend's sporting events, but we were in a conversation with Purdue University about our scheduled football game in West Lafayette. This was complicated because half the conferences in the country were considering playing their games and the other half were not. As it turned out, all collegiate and professional games that weekend were ultimately canceled. We rescheduled the Purdue game for December 1.

On the academic side, we wanted to utilize faculty members who had specializations that could inform a conversation about the events and an evaluation of various public policy follow-throughs. Several teach-ins were organized. On Sunday night, September 16, Student Government arranged a candlelight procession from the Grotto to the reflecting pool in front of Hesburgh Library. A large group participated, and many remarked how moving the occasion was. All the Masses in the dorms that Sunday evening tried to incorporate themes relevant to the unfolding events, and a reflective sense of what we were facing.

In the following week we tried to go on as normally as possible. At the end of the week we would be having our first home football game, against Michigan State, and we wanted to incorporate the national sense of mourning and patriotism into the pregame and half-time ceremonies. NBC decided to televise the whole pregame and some of the half-time events because it was its first major sporting event since September 11. For the pregame ceremonies we had provided everyone in the stadium with American flags on the back of newspapers, and I offered brief reflections and a prayer. At the end of the first quarter, Student Government members and ushers collected money for the family members of the police and firefighters and emergency crews in New York City. The game-day total was $270,000, an amount supplemented by money raised at various Masses and sent in from outside. We were finally able to send almost $330,000 to New York. At half-time the two bands merged and played "'Amazing Grace.'" For many in the stadium, as well as on national television, it was a very moving moment and the highlight of the ceremonies.

In the following week, I made two short trips to Washington, D.C., my first exposure to my home town since September 11. At one moment between duties, I stood on the porch outside my hotel room looking out over the empty Reagan National Airport and one side of the Pentagon. There were no planes to be seen except for one lonely helicopter patrolling up and down the Potomac River. City traffic was rushing by as usual on the interstate approaching the Fourteenth Street Bridge, but I had the sense that everything was different, that there was palpable fear in the air. The hotel staff seemed delighted to have some customers and went out of their way to provide every service.

The next morning I attended a Congressional breakfast at the Russell Office Building on Capitol Hill. Although Congress had recessed the night before, there were still a good number of people present. Security was tight, although this was before the anthrax reports began to surface. Talking to Congressional members and staffers, I got a sense that the government was filled with uncertainty, but also with a steely conviction that they needed to rally together for the common good.

During my second Washington visit, I attended a reception and dinner at the *USA Today* headquarters in Rosslyn, Virginia. From the open deck on top of the building, we could look down on the beautiful vista from the Lincoln Memorial toward the Washington Monument and the Capitol. Our hosts also had two telescopes set up that looked directly into the part of the Pentagon that had been most severely damaged. What a startling contrast between the two scenes. When our bus took a long time getting from Washington to nearby Rosslyn, I wondered what was up. I learned later there had been a bomb threat on Interstate 66, forcing us to skirt the scene to avoid the backup. Such were the signs of the times.

One month to the day after September 11, we held a Blue Mass on campus to honor the police, fire, and emergency crews in Saint Joseph County, where Notre Dame is situated. This followed the tradition in the Catholic Church of the so-called "Month's Mind," that is, the remembrance of the dead one month after the time of their death. When word of our plan got out on the Internet, eleven police and firefighters from New York City who had been directly involved in the events at the World Trade Center decided to join us. They arrived the day the Irish rock band U-2 was scheduled to give a concert in the Joyce Center. U-2 deliberately chose to play at Notre Dame to a more limited audience than they usually command because of the good things they had heard about the school. I had a chance to speak briefly with Bono, their lead singer, and I was impressed with his sincerity and interest in Notre Dame. At the end of the concert they invited the eleven police and firefighters to come up on stage, where they received sustained applause from the concert-goers.

On the day of the Blue Mass, the New York visitors came to my office to present me with a small cross welded out of steel from the World Trade Center buildings. They also brought a flag that had been flying next to the morgue at Ground Zero. The day before they left New York, they had had it blessed by the chaplain, a Franciscan friar who happened to have an undergraduate degree from Notre Dame.

During the visit, one of the police officers told a poignant story. He had been called to the first World Trade Center building hit and had helped people fleeing down the stairs. When building two, the South Tower, collapsed, he found himself trapped with several firefighters and others in a dark hole. Using flashlights, they discovered they were enclosed beneath an iron girder that had snapped in two and was leaning precariously, which ruled out the possibility of using fire axes to try to dig a hole of escape. They went down some stairs looking for another route, but they were convinced they would die.

By some miraculous intervention, he said, they discovered an air pocket that led to light and allowed them to escape the building. At that point the North Tower began to collapse and they all had to run for their lives. As he told me the story, I could see in the faces of the other police and firefighters that all of them were clearly living on the emotional edge.

I was the main celebrant and preacher at the Blue Mass. We had more than a full congregation, and some worshipers stood outside the church. Many of the local police and firefighters attended in uniform, including a color guard from the South Bend Fire Department. We placed the New York police and firefighters in the first pews, and they carried up the gifts to the altar at the preparation time. After Communion, one of the police officers, Sergeant Eddie Colton, accompanied by one of the firefighters, said a few words and then presented the flag they had brought, which I laid before the altar.

After the Mass we had a reception, primarily for the police and firefighters from both the local community and New York. One of the New York officers told me that what impressed him most was that although it took more courage with each passing entry into the stricken buildings to try to help those struggling, no one hesitated, even though they knew their lives were at constant risk, they knew little about what was going on, and there were rumors about further attacks.

Two weeks later I flew to New York City and was met at the airport by the police officer who had spoken at the Blue Mass. It was a beautiful, warm, sunny day as we drove to Saint Vincent's Hospital, the primary place where the World Trade Center victims were brought. Saint Vincent's initially had been overwhelmed by the numbers of victims, especially the burn cases, but soon the victim population disappeared—a foreshadowing of what was to come as the search for further victims turned futile.

From Saint Vincent's we drove past several fire stations fully draped in front and with memorial testimonies on the outside walls. In fact, the fire stations of Manhattan had by then become prime gathering places for locals and visitors trying to make sense of the tragedies. The New York City Fire Department lost 343 firefighters in the World Trade Center—the largest loss of life of any nonmilitary government group in American history. In addition, approximately 60 members of the Port Authority Police, the New York City Police, and a couple of other groups lost their lives. Never before have these departments had to contend with so much personal grieving while at the same time searching for the remains of colleagues and the other victims. Although my visit to New

York City was approximately forty days after September 11, it was almost as if it had all happened yesterday, so vivid were the memories.

We eventually made our way to the First Precinct headquarters, a nondescript building not too far from the World Trade Center site. The precinct includes much of the city's financial district, all the way down to the Battery. Those who patrolled the neighborhood told me over and over that they considered the buildings of the World Trade Center to be the center of the neighborhood, and symbols of the reliability and security of the American financial system. A major event in their recent memory was the 1993 attempt to blow up the Center. That had led to some loss of life and heightened security, but no one imagined anything on the scale they would soon experience.

One officer I met was just back from a long hospital ordeal. He'd had a piece of metal go through his shoulder like a javelin, requiring metal plates in his shoulder and arm. It was clear that he was not going to be able to continue to function as a police officer, and this was weighing heavily on his mind. On the walls of the precinct house were pictures and letters from schoolchildren in New York City and around the country. It only took the reading of a couple of them to turn sad and weepy.

Back in the car, we made our way past Wall Street and almost down to the southern tip of Manhattan and the temporary disaster headquarters adjacent to the World Trade Center. By the time we arrived the sun had set, and the sense of apocalyptic events was overwhelming. We talked to some police from the First Precinct who were staffing the command post and morgue. Some of them had been out to Notre Dame, and many of them were subway alumni fans; the vast majority were Catholic. It went without question that I would have full access to whatever I wanted to see.

First we visited the morgue. Even after all this time they had found the bodies or parts of remains of only about five hundred of those who lost their lives. I can think of few more gruesome duties than to serve in such a place. Once remains are discovered, the workers do the best they can to treat them with dignity and not to become too jaded as days go by.

Eventually, my guide and I put on hard hats and walked around the huge expanse that was now the largest crime scene in the country. The nighttime scene touched all the senses. The acrid smell was persistent and pungent—some combination of metal, human remains, the various materials that had been crushed together, the smoke that continued to come from the burning embers below, and all the toxic substances lying around. The combination of smoke and lights and miasmic clouds reminded one of one of Hieronymus Bosch's medieval portraits of hell. The clanging of gigantic machinery, the movement of trucks carting off steel and other substances, and the hiss of water being sprayed on the mounds were part of the sensory overload. It was hard to remember that forty days' worth of rubble had already been carted off.

The expanse where the two large towers once stood was irregular, so that in one section workers were two stories below the surface while in another they were working on eight or nine or ten stories of steel stretched into the sky. Other structures in the Center complex, four or five stories high, were burned out but untouched. Ringing the whole scene were high-rise buildings, some only slightly damaged, others that probably will never return to their former function.

My guide and I walked down into the depths of the South Tower, Building Two, which was the first to collapse. Large front-end loaders were engaged in their tasks. Gigantic cranes were lifting pieces of steel that weighed tons. Firefighters atop ladder trucks were spraying the areas of greatest smoke. The average temperature beneath the rubble was said to be 1,500°F, and when steel was brought up it was molten and took two or three days to cool down.

Next to each piece of equipment was a member of the police or fire department whose responsibility it was to observe what was being brought to the surface and to identify, if possible, any body parts that might emerge. This was just one stage in the effort to recover evidence; once the accumulated debris was carried to the landfill in Staten Island, two hundred people raked through it non-stop seeking out additional evidence.

While we were standing in the middle of Building Two, a fire chief came up from below and paused to chat. He described, in retrospect, some of the deficiencies of the towers' construction. The designers had eliminated much of the structural steel previously used in such buildings in favor of more modern methods of construction, and he theorized that this eliminated one level of protection against collapse. In addition, he said, the stairwells were too narrow, so that when firefighters were going up, only one person at a time could come down. With all the occupants trying to escape simultaneously, it jammed the routes of exit.

He also acknowledged that at some point it became suicidal to continue rescue efforts because the chance of collapse increased with each passing moment. He said most firefighters would have been aware of the danger and yet made the decision to continue with their task. In a sense, people watching television at the time of the disaster knew more than those on the scene—and in an age of instant communication, this should not be surprising. A number of the police and firefighters with whom I spoke described their great fear that we were either at war or that further devastating incidents were in store. When Mayor Rudolph Giuliani and the surviving leadership of the police and fire departments were able to reestablish a command structure and a system of communication, it made all the difference in the world.

Toward the end of our conversation, the fire chief heard over his radio that his crew had found the remains of a woman, and he went to join them. I stood silently at a distance as the crew uncovered the remains. From what I could see, they had most of a body. They placed it on a stretcher and covered it with a flag, then sent it off to the morgue. Someone came down to the area and played taps, a haunting sound in such a location.

The people working at the site had a certain resentment about the area becoming a tourist attraction. But, judging from my experience, much of the nation and the world needs to discover and rediscover the human dimension of this tragedy. I felt the same way at the World Trade Center as I have felt at the battlefields of Gettysburg or Chancellorsville or Manassas/Bull Run: This is indeed sacred ground, and we honor the dead by being present at the place where they lost their lives.

EUROPE

IRELAND

On a sunny October day, my two sisters, my brother-in-law, and I undertook a search for the Malloy family roots in the neighborhood of Castlebar, in the part of Ireland known as "the West." Our search was prompted by my discovery, during an earlier visit to the area, of a tombstone with the Malloy name.

From Castlebar we drove a short distance to Graffymore, a village with a few houses but no obvious center, then took a branch road into the countryside, passing undulating hills, rocks, heather, and bog fields with a small stream flowing through them. When we got out of the car for a picture, it was absolutely silent. In the distance was Croagh Patrick, the mountain where Saint Patrick is buried. This seemed to be the Ur-site, the most primitive place of origin, for the Malloy clan.

I felt I had come home.

In search of the church and graveyard, we stopped at a school that had recently celebrated its one-hundredth anniversary. Saint Patrick's National School, Cornanool, was an Irish version of the little red schoolhouse. The kids were absolutely gorgeous and quite curious about us. The teachers brought out some handwritten logbooks, preserved from the school that preceded this one, that dated back to the 1870s.

Here is what we found: 1874, Katherine Mulloy, age six; 1879, John Mulloy, landowner, eventually left school to work at home; 1878, Edward Mulloy, age seven, left school in 1884 to work at home; 1880, Willy Mulloy, age six; 1906, Agnes Mulloy, age six, went to America in 1907; 1883, Walter Mulloy, age six. The fact that the name was spelled with a "u" is not significant; Malloy, Molloy, and Mulloy are almost interchangeable, because the stateside spelling of immigrants' names often depended on the whim of immigration authorities. Some time before our trip, a genealogist traced the four sides of our family back to the passage from Europe and discovered that many families from this region of Ireland had settled in Scranton, Pennsylvania, about the time my grandparents did. We took the evidence from the school's logbooks as confirmation of that.

Our hunt took us next to a cemetery beside the remains of an old church with a sign saying it was built in the thirteenth century and had served as a hideout for a group of rebels in 1798. One of the predominant names on the tombstones was O'Malley, and one stone next to the church was either O'Malley or O'Malloy. It's an open question whether the Mulloys whose names were listed in the school records would have had enough money for such a display; I am of the conviction they would not. Yet I was struck once again in that solitary spot by the raw beauty of the surroundings and the eloquent testimony of those lives, which likely included some of my ancestors. As we left the area, a beautiful rainbow was visible. Who doesn't believe in miracles or signs from heaven?

That "homecoming" occurred in 1996, a couple of years after I had proposed to my sisters, Mary Long and Joanne Rorapaugh, that we spend some time touring around our ancestral island. We were sure our mother would be worried about all three of her children being abroad at the same time, but pleased that we could do it together. Because I had to be in Ireland as part of the official Notre Dame party for our 1996 football game against Navy in Dublin, it seemed a good time to piggy-back the family tour.

It was the fourth of more than a half-dozen trips I've taken to Ireland. When I made the first visit in 1991, at the age of fifty, to the land of three-quarters of my genealogical roots (the other fourth being English), I admit to having felt a sense of romance and excitement. If asked what nationality I am, I instinctively say American, and I incline toward a world identity as well. But there is no way to disavow my family roots and my family history. My sense of belonging was reinforced the day I arrived on that initial visit when I drove from Shannon via Ennis and Gort and Galway to Clifden on the Atlantic Ocean. Most of the faces I encountered I had seen before—my relatives in Scranton, certain crowds in Chicago, New York, or Boston, a portion of the students at every freshman orientation weekend. In Ireland, I found, you recognize everyone but do not know anyone.

Walking around the coastline city of Westport on that trip, I got really emotional when I spotted Mulloy's Pub and Molloy's Hardware Store. In a small souvenir shop, I bought a music box with a scene on top that proclaimed "Molloy's Pub." Perhaps, I mused, my roots are to be found in the tavern business.

My first impressions of western Ireland have been reinforced many times over. One impression is of stones,

stones, stones—the countryside is an endless line of stone fences three or four feet high. Originally, stones were gathered to clear the fields so that some minimum agriculture could take place, then used to make fences, but the art of shaping stone fences, generally without mortar, is a characteristic of the region. There's a saying about the region that goes: "There are more rocks than sheep, more sheep than cows, more cows than people." This is true. Every village also has its Catholic church, and one frequently sees religious statues and Celtic crosses. The scenery, though severe at times, is spectacularly beautiful and enchanting.

For Irish-Americans, the key decade of Irish history was the 1840s, the years of the potato famine. The total population of Ireland then was eight million; today it is five million (three and a half million in the Republic, one and a half in the North). More than forty million Americans claim some degree of Irish descent.

Americans who drive in Ireland find getting used to the left side of the highway challenging at first, especially in the West, where paved-over cow paths run between stone walls on both sides. But driving is okay once you get in the groove. In the roundabouts, the car on the inside has all the rights and you just hope some dumb American does not come along before learning that rule.

Ireland's Ring of Kerry is one of the best known tourist areas in Europe, combining dramatic seascapes with rolling mountain heights and gentle valleys, but the main

Ring highway winds a lot and is a challenge to drivers, especially in the summer season when the tourist buses barely squeeze around the sharp curves. Large signs warn drivers to beware of the buses but don't tell you what to do when you encounter one. One day I got a flat tire because a bus forced me into a rock by the edge of the road.

Blarney Castle and the Blarney Stone are a favorite stopping place for Americans. Kissing the stone gives you the gift of gab, tradition says, and since gab is indispensable for university officers, I had to do it. To kiss the stone, you lie on your back and hold yourself steady while you lean down and make contact with the bottom of the stone, which is one of the walls on the top floor of the castle with no roof and open to the sky. Kissing the stone also symbolizes the ritual return to Ireland for those with Irish blood.

The Rock of Cashel, known from about A.D. 370 as "Cashel of the Kings," is one of the most famous spots in Ireland. Saint Patrick visited the site around 450 and baptized the reigning Munster king. The ancient fortress affords a commanding view of the surrounding area, and one sees green, green, green everywhere, especially in clear sunlight after a heavy rain.

The part of County Clare called the Burren is a plateau with heavy rock concentrations and considerable prehistoric remains that occupies a vast area in Ireland's western mountains. Nearby are the Cliffs of Moher, one of the most renowned points of beauty in all Ireland. They are almost sheer on the water side, with vertical drops of hundreds of feet. Colonies of sea birds nest in caves and holes of the cliff sides.

Connemara is the peninsula in western Ireland that lies south of Westport and north of Galway, with Clifdon on its western tip. I urge Connemara visitors to stop at Kylemore Abbey, a nineteenth-century castle that was taken over by a group of Benedictine nuns in 1921 as a private girls' boarding school. It was built on a spectacular site, with mountains behind, its own large lake in front, and other mountains in the distance, and it has survived neglect and a large fire.

One amusing stop I made during a drive through Connemara was in the middle of nowhere, where a plaque on a monument in a parking lot proudly proclaimed, "On this site in 1897 nothing happened."

Dublin, on the eastern side of the island, is one of Europe's oldest capital cities, tracing its roots back to a Viking settlement. In 1591, Queen Elizabeth I founded Trinity College to "civilize" the Irish and keep them from the influence of "popery." The best-preserved areas of the city today go back to the Georgian period of the eighteenth century, when elegant private homes and great public buildings were constructed. The 1916 insurrection and the War of Independence that followed led to the destruction of much of the city's center.

Dublin Castle, however, is in exquisite condition, since the Irish government paid for extensive renovations related to using the facility for the European Community meetings. For much of the last two centuries, the castle was the seat of the British government in Ireland and a hostile place for my Catholic ancestors. When my sisters and I stopped at the castle, we kidded that any previous members of our families who might have been there had probably been either in chains or on the way to punishment.

NORTHERN IRELAND

On my first visit to Belfast in 1991, it appeared that the Catholic and Protestant strife was confined to what we would call inner-city neighborhoods, though in Belfast's case they are more on the city's periphery. I saw curbstones painted in the colors of the IRA (the Irish Republican Army), large-scale graffiti with IRA slogans, boundary walls with barbed wire on top, and frequent squads of British military on patrol with rifles pointed at passing cars. It was all clearly intended to be intimidating. In the Protestant slum neighborhoods the colors and graffiti were different but the result was the same, except that there were few army patrols.

Yet in most of Belfast, life seemed totally undisturbed. The downtown was full of shoppers and workers, and in the neutral neighborhoods life was as it might be anywhere else in Ireland. Belfast, I concluded, was not Beirut, although the international perception at the time was that there were strong comparisons: the violence and entrenched attitudes and practices were not to be underestimated.

My second crossing of the border into Northern Ireland a year later was less emotionally startling. Armed soldiers and police either checked drivers or waved them through. On the sides of the road were pillboxes with machine guns sticking out, and on the hills above were other pillboxes and communications antennae. Three or four helicopters were flying in the vicinity of the border— all this despite a relative lull in the violence. This was no game they were playing.

Before 1917, of course, all of Ireland was subject to British rule, and the country was one of the regions of Great Britain, like Wales and Scotland. With the uprising of 1917, Ireland achieved a degree of self-rule. When the Republic was created, there were two broad political groups: the Nationalists, who wanted the whole island to be separated from British rule, and the Unionists, who wanted England and Ireland to remain politically con- nected. Unionist sentiment was strongest in the six coun- ties of Ulster, but only four of the six had a majority of Unionists, and those four became today's Northern Ireland.

To maintain control, the government of Northern Ireland imposed discriminatory policies against the minority Nationalists, most of whom were also Catholic. After the American civil rights movement received world- wide attention in the 1960s, a comparable movement among the Nationalists in Northern Ireland began to push for civil rights legislation with regard to employment, housing, and voting rights. Because the police were largely Protestant and Unionist, the Nationalists met with violent suppression, either directly by the police or pas- sively through police tolerance of hoodlum actions. On the Nationalist side, this led to a revival of the Irish

Republican Army, which had disbanded after the uprising earlier in the century. The IRA became the voice and action arm of militant nationalism, or Republicanism. The corresponding group on the Protestant side is the Loyalists, who also practice violent means.

From the 1960s, British troops were involved in interventions between the two sides. At first they were welcomed by the Catholics as more reliable than the local police, but over time they came to be seen as part of a British effort to scuttle the move toward fuller participation by Catholics in power in the North.

Although the terms Nationalist and Unionist are used interchangeably with the terms Catholic and Protestant respectively, the reality is much more complex. Many militants on both sides have not been inside a church for years, except to attend the funerals of dead colleagues. Furthermore, the greatest levels of militancy tend to be found in neighborhoods where the unemployment rate is highest. In that sense, one could say that the persistence of the conflict has more to do with economics than religion. Belfast tends to be the city where the struggle is most visible, but even so there are large parts of that city where the residents sound like American suburbanites lamenting inner-city problems.

Who are the members of the IRA? They are a group with large caches of bomb-making material and other arms, probably financed by bank robberies, protection money, drug deals, contributions from sympathizers, and donations from such overseas groups as Irish Northern Aid (NORAID) a U.S. front for the IRA. They have fully embraced the tactics of guerrilla theory, which include working in cells so that no more than one operation at a time can be exposed. Some believe that the majority of IRA members are dedicated revolutionaries who embrace the romantic songs that celebrate past Irish rebel exploits. Others consider them a criminal syndicate that cannot afford peace since it would pauperize them and leave them with no serviceable skills.

During a 1996 visit to Ulster, my party drove from Belfast to Derry, which is that city's official name now even though the Unionists still call it Londonderry and the county is named Londonderry on maps. Derry is the port city from which many Irish emigrants sailed to the United States and Canada during the potato famine. We took a driving tour through the Bogside neighborhood, Derry's Catholic ghetto, and saw a stone memorial commemorating the nearly twenty people who were killed by British troops on so-called "Bloody Sunday" in 1974, the real beginning of the worst part of the troubles. Once again we saw wall graffiti celebrating the IRA and damning the British.

BRITAIN

In 1995, I celebrated the twenty-fifth anniversary of my ordination to the priesthood with a trip through Wales and Scotland, beginning in County Devon in the southeast corner of England. Exeter, the county seat, has been the capital of the region since the Romans established a fortress there two thousand years ago, and right outside my hotel was a remnant of Roman city walls going back to A.D. 200. At the heart of Exeter is the great Gothic cathedral of Saint Peter, begun in 1275, whose 300-foot stretch of unbroken Gothic vaulting, rising from a forest of ribbed columns, is the longest in the world.

In Crediton I visited a cathedral built on the site of an ancient church named after Saint Boniface, who was born there about A.D. 680. Boniface was the missionary bishop who carried Christianity to the Germanic tribes of the Continent. He is identified with the felling of the sacred oak tree of Geismar, thereby challenging the authority of the local gods.

The famous port of Plymouth is Devon's largest city and the port from which the Pilgrims embarked on the *Mayflower* in 1620. Plymouth was also the embarkation point for the journeys of Sir Francis Drake and for the settlers of Newfoundland.

For me, Buckfastleigh, the site of a Catholic Benedictine monastery called Buckfast Abbey, proved to be one of those pleasant surprises that travel often provides. It is a community of monks about a half-mile off a major highway in a beautiful, serene green setting that exudes a sense of timelessness and contemplation. The original monastery on the site was founded in A.D. 1018. In 1539 it was dissolved by Henry VIII, but rebuilding was begun in 1882 and today the abbey includes the main church and the monastery grounds, as well as a large cafeteria, a gift shop, and a retreat center. The monks are famous for bee-keeping, tonic wine, and wool. (Despite my nickname, I have never felt the calling to become a monk.)

Wales is a once-independent country that is now part of Britain. It is a solid block of land on the middle-western coast of the British Isles, largely mountainous, with a plethora of medieval castles and ruined abbeys but only a handful of cities. The Welsh are a Celtic race whose people were never Romanized or Anglicized. Not until the reign of King Edward I (1272–1307) was English supremacy established in the region. Henry VIII tried to abolish the Welsh language, but a Welsh translation of the Bible authorized by Elizabeth I ensured its survival. The language today is spoken by only 20 percent of the population.

York, the military capital of Roman Britain, gets an A-plus from me as a tourist site. Following the fall of the Roman Empire in the fifth century, a Saxon town grew up over the ruins of the Roman fort. On Christmas Eve A.D. 627, the Northumbrian King Edwin introduced Christianity to the area by being baptized in a little wooden church. In the ninth century, the Viking conquerors made York their English capital. In the Middle Ages, York became an important trade center and inland port on the River Ouse. Today the Archbishop of York is second only to the Archbishop of Canterbury in the hierarchy of the Church of England. The cathedral is one of the four or five most beautiful I have ever seen.

Edinburgh, Scotland's capital city, is built on seven hills. From atop one of them, a crag of hard, black volcanic rock formed during the Ice Age, Edinburgh Castle watches over the city. Below the castle, the Old and New Towns stretch out, bordered by a long expanse of North

Sea inlet called the Firth of Forth. Within the castle are the eleventh-century Saint Margaret's Chapel and the crown room containing the Scottish crown, scepter, and sword.

Despite the national reputation for Scottish reserve and a rather severe view of human nature, the young Scots on the prowl in Edinburgh on the Friday night I was there could have been young people anywhere. Their outfits were fashionable—whether fashionable mod or fashionable grunge. It is a universal trait of human nature that all young people, in rebellion against the standards of forced conformity, dress exactly alike within two or three modes, whether in Beijing or Mexico City, Paris or Chicago.

From Edinburgh, it takes about one and a half hours to drive to Saint Andrews, the birthplace of golf and a mecca for golfers from every continent. The holes run straight, and there are no water hazards or real hills, but the fairways are narrow and the brush along the sides is higher than in regular courses. The biggest problem is said to be the crosswind from the sea.

Anything north of Edinburgh is like the north woods of Michigan or the lower levels of the Rockies: irregular terrain with wide valleys amid mountains that were carved by glaciers during the Ice Age. Fir trees predominate, and swift-running streams and rivers are plentiful. Inverness, the famous staging point for trips to the Scottish highlands, is located in a part of Scotland that gets five months of snow and supports a busy ski season in winter. During my visit there I walked to the Ness River and eventually reached the old Inverness castle that sits on a high hill next to the main drag. The castle is now a government building, but the area around it is a park with a nice overlook on the river, the town, and the hills on the other side.

In the western part of Scotland there are interlocking lakes, all roughly the same shape. Loch Ness is one of them, long and fairly narrow and 700 feet deep, with mountains on either side that are often cloaked in wisps of mist and cloud. The small towns in that region contain bed-and-breakfast homes and small eating places. While I was having lunch at a five-table restaurant one day, two Scottish girls were playing Motown sounds on the jukebox. The waitress came by to make sure the noise wasn't bothering my group; I think I surprised her when I said we liked it.

My visits to England have included several stays in London, a city that has become visibly multiracial. That is reflected not only in the people you see on the streets but also in the public employees, shopkeepers, and hotel and restaurant workers. In a sense, this diversity is one of the fruits of empire and of the ease of entry that characterized it. I know from my reading that there is some neighborhood segregation, especially in the poorer areas of London, and that outbreaks of hostility and violence occur periodically. But in the new Europe, particularly in cities like London, Paris, Rome, and Berlin, there can be no return to the relative racial uniformity of the past. Like the United States, we are all in this together, for better or worse.

During one of my visits to London I resided at Lambeth Palace, the London office and home of the Archbishop of

Canterbury, titular head of the Anglican Communion around the world and the closest equivalent to the Pope that exists on the Protestant side of things—although Anglicans often avoid the term "Protestant." Lambeth Palace has been the London home of Canterbury archbishops since 1197. Morton's Tower and Gate stand at its entrance, and a porter grants entry to the grounds. The archbishop and his wife live in a modest but adequate flat on the top floor, and the rest of the building includes guest rooms, offices, and meeting places. On the walls throughout are grand-scale portraits of the previous archbishops, of which there have been more than one hundred. Among them were Thomas Cranmer, who composed the Book of Common Prayer, and Thomas Becket, who was murdered in Canterbury Cathedral in the twelfth century. Rumor has it that after Archbishop William Laud's picture was hung in 1645 it fell unexpectedly from the wall, and a week later he was executed. Ever since, the pictures have been reinforced as they were hung.

London is an intriguing place that I still find fascinating after several visits. The streets seldom go in a straight line, but meander according to some ancient vision, probably the favorite routes of cows and sheep. The Thames defines the most historic districts as it curves and turns. The streets are full at night, and there is a lively theater, restaurant, and pub scene. For all the city's traffic, London drivers retain the British sense of decorum. The intersections, at least in the heavy tourist areas, have signs on the sidewalks reminding you which way to look for oncoming traffic—enough visitors have been maimed or killed to warrant this precaution.

A visit to England in the mid-1990s to attend the Oxford International Roundtable on Education Policy gave me my first opportunity to see Oxford, though I had previously toured Cambridge University. Oxford is more urban than Cambridge—it began rather piecemeal as a loose confederation of independent colleges, which partly accounts for its dispersions through the city of Oxford. Cambridge, by contrast, was begun by a group of faculty from Oxford who wanted a more coherent university and a more isolated and planned campus.

There are forty colleges at Oxford, the first five founded in the thirteenth century and the most recent in 1966. The buildings vary in elaborateness, charm, sources of support, tradition, and beauty. When a student applies to Oxford, he or she is asked to indicate three top choices for college; it is then up to the colleges to make the decision. The tutorial tradition lives on at Oxford—in each course the grade hinges entirely on a final exam that is both written and oral. If a student is going to goof off, it's best done at the beginning of the term.

The dining halls have a "high table" where faculty members sit for a formal dinner most evenings. Students can choose to eat at an early, informal dinner or a later formal dinner at which robes are worn. All the colleges are coed today, although Somerville College was exclusively female for much of its history; Margaret Thatcher went there, which hasn't hurt fund-raising efforts. As you go from college to college, you'll hear about the famous alumni of each, but it is difficult to remember which names go with which college. (I am sure that within the Oxford–Cambridge axis it would be a sin to admit this, like saying Joe Montana went to Southern Cal.)

A side trip to Blenheim Palace introduced me to one of the great country houses and estates of England. The palace covers seven acres, has 320 rooms, and is surrounded by 2,700 acres of courtyards, formal gardens, and parkland. Winston Churchill was born there (by accident, since his American mother gave birth prematurely), and it contains a display of Churchillian letters, outfits, and speeches. The family of the present Duke of Marlborough lives in one part of the palace, but the rest of the property is open to the public (which is, of course, the primary method of paying for its upkeep). Having been to Versailles, I felt Blenheim could hold its own, even though its scale is smaller.

FRANCE

I love Paris. Each time I'm there I am struck anew by how extraordinarily beautiful the core area of the city is. It survived World War II intact, but, even more important, successive French governments have given it the attention and money it deserves. How bad it makes the plight of my home city, Washington, D.C., seem; to have had the capital of a nation in financial receivership is a disgrace.

The French have a sense of style in their dress and of civility in the way they carry themselves. The city's rooftops are infinitely intriguing; viewed horizontally from upper-story windows, they are a tangle of chimney tops, television aerials, pink decorative devices, weather vanes, metalwork, flower gardens, and the like.

It is hard to have a bad meal in Paris. At lunch in a small Parisian bistro during one of my visits, the tables were crowded together but the food was excellent and the walls were covered with Toulouse-Lautrec-type posters. The ambiance was authentic and the conversation lively. Parisians love their sidewalk cafes, and so do I; they are great for people-watching and for feeling one is part of a wider community.

Unlike the United States, the wealth of Paris tends to be concentrated within the city limits and a few suburbs. The ring around the city, called the Red Zone, is where the poor are concentrated, and many of them are from Islamic countries and Africa. Much of the city's crime, especially violent crime, takes place there.

The etiquette for Paris drivers is "the rule of the right," which seems to mean pay no attention to whomever is on your left—just look right and yield if necessary. With boulevards that can sometimes be twelve lanes across, negotiating the frequently occurring traffic circles with multiple streets entering them is a real challenge.

Versailles, the famous palace headquarters of King Louis XIV and one of the great estates of the world, was at one time larger than the present city limits of Paris. This huge palace was intended in scale and splendor to impress representatives of foreign powers with the glory and power of France. The chapel reflects the hierarchy of the time, which tried implicitly or explicitly to render Louis XIV as the equivalent of an apostle of Christ. The great Hall of Mirrors was the special greeting place for foreign diplomats. The palace is surrounded by one park that descends from the Chateau to the Grand Canal, a second large park, and the Trianon gardens and museums.

The American Embassy in Paris resembles a small-scale Versailles, with large, high-ceilinged rooms full of paintings, mirrors, and art pieces, and a lovely interior garden park. Thomas Jefferson and Benjamin Franklin were among the first American representatives to France.

The bullet train from Paris to Lyon averages 150 miles an hour, and the trip takes exactly two hours. The second-largest city of France, Lyon was a major center during the Roman Empire and at various times afterward. The architecture combines elements of both northern and southern Europe, and many buildings have red tile roofs, which you never see in Paris. On one side of the city is a high hill with a prominent nineteenth-century basilica that was built in thanksgiving to our Lady for protecting the town from the Black Plague in the seventeenth century and from the Prussian army in the War of 1870.

Cardes, a fortress town in the Midi-Pyrenees mountains, has been called one of the best unknown towns of Europe. It's built along the sides and top of a high hill, with stonework walls, brick streets, and a flat area on top with outdoor restaurants. The effect is spectacularly beautiful.

Albi, not far from Cardes, was the center of the Cathar or Albigensian movement, a lay-led thirteenth-century reform movement with strong ascetic tendencies. It was the site of bloody conflicts when the Vatican declared the Albigensians heretics and ordered a crusade against them. Present-day Albi is a peaceful city with an art gallery devoted to Toulouse-Lautrec.

GERMANY

A Berlin tour I took in 1993, less than four years after the fall of Communism and the rejoining of East and West Germany, included a visit to the Brandenburg Gate and the Pariser Platz, the site of the Berlin Wall that for so long divided East and West Berlin. By then it was wide open again, with few signs of the wall remaining. Near the Brandenburg Gate is the Reichstag Building, where Hitler used to harangue the crowds. In the rear is a simple memorial to those who lost their lives trying to escape past the wall into West Berlin. The youngest listed was thirteen years old, and the oldest was eighty. It is hard to contemplate all the arrogance and display of military power that Berlin saw in the twentieth century. World War I and World War II were waged from there, and during the Cold War the city was a pivotal place of resistance against Communism. Berlin was effectively destroyed at the end of World War II, and rebuilt only to suffer division and a thermonuclear face-off.

Where did Hitler come from? How could a country

with such deep religious roots in Catholicism and Lutheranism have been the center of the Holocaust against the Jews? In the wake of the unification of the two Berlins and the two Germanys, one must also wonder about the appeal of the Russian brand of Communism— an ideology that emerged out of the theoretical speculations of Karl Marx in the London Library and that led to the deaths of millions of people, the suppression of civil liberties, the imposition of a police state, the persecution of organized religion, and the creation of a massive, ineffective government bureaucracy.

Some felt there would be a great revival of religion in East Germany after reunification, but not much happened. Perhaps the churches were not properly prepared. The same human yearnings were there, but alternate value systems were propounded by advertising, television, rock music, and popular culture in general. The Good News is not alien to all the glitz and seductive quality of affluence and leisure, but it needs to revitalize popular culture. Sometimes the primary American exports seem to be violent movies, television sit-coms, rap music and hard rock, jeans, and logo baseball caps and T-shirts. This is not a lot to be proud of.

The hopeful things I saw on that visit were people from different cultural backgrounds enjoying a summer day in the city. Turkish families were barbecuing in the park; thousands of young people were cycling or walking; the police were present but inactive; and a great calm and sense of mutual tolerance prevailed. Not too far away, Sarajevo and other cities were being blown apart that year, but in Berlin, the scene of countless war movies, spy thrillers, and newsreels of goose-stepping soldiers, there was promise that the new Europe may indeed succeed.

Cologne is famous for its home-brewed beer—something that seems to be a point of pride for every region of Germany. The huge, Gothic Cologne Cathedral was begun in the twelfth century and completed in the nineteenth. Despite some damage in World War II, it has been well renovated. It contains the oldest medieval crucifix and extensive stained-glass windows from just about every era. There is a special devotion to the Three Magi, and a gold-plated case in the cathedral purports to contain the bones of the Magi.

I instinctively liked Munich. Although it was extensively damaged in the war, the oldest part of the city has been rebuilt in a traditional way, with wide walking plazas and no cars. One can watch the glockenspiel go through its motions at 11:00 A.M. daily. I estimated there were ten Catholic churches, including the cathedral, near Marienplatz, the town center.

In terms of sheer natural beauty, the Bavarian Alps district ranks with the Greek Isles, the West Coast of Ireland, and the foothills of the Rockies. The people who live there are obviously prosperous, the farms are in good shape, and the towns are clean and flower-filled. Many of the homes have paintings on the side depicting religious or natural scenes, and there are shrines and crucifixes at the waysides.

ABOARD THE *SEA CLOUD II*

In the summer of 2001, I was part of a Notre Dame group of trustees, members of various college advisory councils, administrators, and staff members that visited eight countries on a cruise aboard the *Sea Cloud II*, a ninety-six-passenger sailing ship. London was our jumping-off place, and the adventure began on a medium-size transport boat. Our route was London to Bayeux/Caen in France, to Honfleur in France, to Bruges (Belgium), to Amsterdam (the Netherlands), to Heligoland Island (Germany), to Kristiansand (Norway), to Helsingborg (Sweden), and finally to Copenhagen (Denmark).

During the first night, our ship came into Bayeux and proceeded through locks to Caen, where tugs brought us to our mooring place. Buses took our group to the Normandy coast to view the site of the D day invasion. We went first to Arromanches, a small seaside town where a port was created in the midst of the Allied landing so supplies could reach the troops as they moved inland. This area was entrusted to British and Canadian forces. The American troops came ashore just to the south on what were called, at the time, Omaha Beach and Utah Beach.

From Arromanches we bused over to the American Cemetery, and it was a deeply moving experience for all of us. The entrance has pale-green, manicured lawns, a visitors' center, a memorial area at one end, and a chapel at the other. In between are endless rows of white crosses or uprights with stars of David. Buried there are only those whose families did not ask for the remains to be returned to the States, plus those whose identities are unknown. We could look below and see the beaches and the North Sea, and an eerie silence hung over the place. I would have liked more private time at the cemetery.

Eating dinner back on the ship that evening, we were pulled by tugs through the Caen Canal to the sea. Because it was Saturday night, crowds were lined up along the way to watch our passage. I'm sure we appeared to be the height of romantic, elegant adventure.

We docked next in Honfleur, an old port on the northern coast of Normandy, and walked to the tenth-century Church of Saint Catherine for Mass. Honfleur is a fishing village framed by sloping hills opposite the water and an interior lagoon or marina where small boats sit at harbor. It was the birthplace of Impressionism because it was a quick train ride from Paris and offered access to the sea.

Before our stop at Bruges, we had a lecture on Michelangelo's Bruges Madonna, a sculpture in the Church of Notre Dame. Commissioned by a wealthy Bruges merchant, it was carved in 1503, two years after the *David* was presented to great acclaim in Florence. Michelangelo had a deep devotion to the Virgin, and the image of Mary in the Bruges Madonna is quite young, suggesting that she is the first among the disciples, or perpetually young as a virgin. Jesus is pictured as stepping down toward the viewer. We visited the Church of Our Lady to view the Michelangelo sculpture *in situ*. It proved just as lovely as our lecturer had promised.

Within sight of the German island of Heligoland, the

wind died and our boat just sat there—a reminder of the pitfalls of sea travel in the past, when there were no engines to fall back on in a calm. We were picked up by tenders, which brought us from our berthing place, about five miles offshore, to the island. None of us had ever heard of this island, which is located somewhere between Germany, England, and Denmark. Originally a medieval pirate stronghold and later a British property, the island was eventually traded to Germany in a swap for Zanzibar. During both world wars Heligoland served as a strategic German naval base for submarines and aircraft. Toward the end of World War II, it was devastated by Allied bombing. Now it is a resort and tourist mecca, catering primarily to a German clientele.

After a stop at Kristiansand, Norway, we sailed into Helsingborg to much fanfare, not only because our sailing ship always attracted attention, but also because ours was the first cruise ship to dock at a new pier designed specifically for such landings. As we neared the harbor, a helicopter was circling the ship taking video shots, and a fireboat was shooting off an arc of water. Once we were tied up, a local teenage band performed.

A six-hundred-year-old watchtower affords a nice view of the harbor, and one can see across the water to the castle at Elsinore, Denmark, the setting for *Hamlet*. Helsingborg is the center of southern Sweden, an area that serves as the breadbasket of the country. In some winters it never snows or drops below freezing—in sharp contrast to the far north of Norway, near the Arctic Circle.

ICELAND

On my flight home after the *Sea Cloud* cruise I stopped in Iceland, a country with a unique geological history, and the place where Leif Eriksson was born. Eleven percent of the island is covered by glaciers, including Vatnajökull, the largest glacier in Europe and a hot spot of volcanic and geothermal activity. Thirty postglacial volcanoes have erupted in the past ten centuries, and natural hot water supplies cheap, pollution-free heating. Rivers provide inexpensive hydroelectric power.

Iceland's standard of living is high, with a per capita income that is among the best in the world. Most people live on the coast, since the interior is uninhabitable, and about half the population lives in the capital, Reykjavik, and its suburbs. Because Iceland is so close to the Arctic Circle, there are three to four hours of sun in December and twenty-four hours of sun in June. The air and water are clear and unpolluted, and the only pollution comes from autos.

I saw some houses that go back to the Viking era. The island became Christian in A.D. 1000. At Skalholt Church the last two Catholic bishops of Iceland were martyred on orders of the King of Denmark. The Plains of Parliament is the tectonic spot where Europe and the Americas are moving apart. Although the last earthquake occurred a year before my visit, pressure was reported building again for a big one. I stopped at Geysir (from which the term "geyser" derives). You can stand right next to these geysers and watch them spout spontaneously into the air. Some reach 250°C. At a viewing point above a two-stage waterfall—not quite as big as Niagara, but impressive— I could see one of the large glaciers in the distance.

Iceland has much to recommend it. It is beautiful, safe, easy to get to, and a geological wonder. Reykjavik is an interesting, walkable capital city with oodles of restaurants and many museums, and everyone speaks English. You can bicycle around, or hike if you wish. I do not recommend visiting in December, though, unless you have a problem with the sun.

◙

THE
MEDITERRANEAN
REGION

THE HOLY LAND

My first trip to Israel was in 1979, when I was still a staff member at Moreau Seminary and teaching in Notre Dame's theology department. I went there with a biblical study group of about forty, and we operated out of Nazareth for one week and out of Jerusalem for two. That time in the Holy Land had a profound impact on my teaching, preaching, and sense of biblical history, topography, and culture.

It was fifteen years before my second visit, this time to attend meetings regarding Notre Dame's Ecumenical Institute for Theological Studies, which is located at Tantur in Jerusalem. Tantur, as the Institute is called for short, is a beautiful hilltop facility on a major transportation route between Jerusalem and Bethlehem. The property is owned by the Vatican, but the building was constructed by monies raised by Ted Hesburgh at the request of Pope Paul VI, who wanted an institute in the Holy Land where scholars of Judaism, Christianity, and Islam could gather for research and dialogue. Notre Dame administers the facility.

At 4:00 A.M. on my first morning at Tantur, the local Muslim began chanting praise to Allah over an outdoor speaker. It lasted about ten minutes, then all was quiet again. The night sky was still dark except for a full moon, and I stood for a while on the balcony of my room. It was a romantic first morning in Jerusalem.

After dinner that evening, we went up to Tantur's roof on a beautiful night with a soft breeze blowing. Below on the road to Bethlehem was an Israeli army checkpoint, set up to prevent Palestinians without work permits from entering Jerusalem. Meanwhile, a few feet away, a steady stream of Palestinians was cutting through the fields on their way home. The workers, most of them middle-aged men supporting families, never know when the soldiers will hide behind the walls to catch them.

On a couple of mornings during my stay at Tantur, a single helicopter flew over, presumably to survey the checkpoint and the border area. One hovered over the area for forty-five minutes as the soldiers hassled Palestinians going to work, chasing them back toward Bethlehem. It was a sad game, since a couple of hundred had already gone through the Tantur property.

During the 1991 Gulf War, Tantur's roof was a good spot to watch Scud missiles heading for Tel Aviv, and Patriots being fired from around Jerusalem. Because Jerusalem is a sacred city to Muslims, everyone doubted that it would be targeted, but there was still a sense of pain.

On one side of the Tantur property is a tunnel carrying the road from Gilo, a Jewish neighborhood, to one of the Jewish settlements on the West Bank. The road's only purpose is to allow the settlers to go back and forth without having to pass through any Palestinian villages. In the Middle East everything is amazingly close. At night from Bethlehem you can see across to Amman, the capital of Jordan. Israel/Palestine happens to be at the meeting point of all the passageways on land in this part of the world. That is its blessing and its curse.

Because Jerusalem is a sacred city to Jews, Christians, and Muslims alike, it is full of memories and deep feelings. Christians constitute about 2.5 percent of the population of Israel/Palestine, and the percentage is going down—which is a source of great concern. The Christian Arabs tend to leave the country for advanced education and economic opportunities and never return; they feel squeezed between the Muslims and the Jews. Theologically it would be disastrous if there were no real Christian presence in the Holy Land. Although various Christian groups own a considerable amount of land in the region, what is missing is the practicing community; pilgrims simply are not enough.

I had an interesting conversation at Tantur with a Palestinian Christian woman from Ramallah in the West Bank. She was well educated and hungry for intellectual exchange, but in order to come to Tantur she had to get a special pass and be out of town by sunset. She spoke of her disappointment that so few of the 800,000 Christian tourists each year make any effort to learn about the local Christian communities, and she expressed fears that the sacred Christian shrines in the Holy Land could become museums instead of places of active worship if the Arab Christian population is not supported.

A Christian community has been in Jerusalem since the first Pentecost. The era of pilgrimages brought people from elsewhere, and many monasteries were established in the Judean desert. After the Council of Chalcedon in 451, several of the churches no longer recognized the authority of the Archbishop of Jerusalem. Later, the Crusaders made one of their bishops the Latin Patriarchate of Jerusalem, though he was never accepted by the local church. In the fifteenth century, the Franciscans assumed responsibility for the holy places, and nineteenth-century Christian missionaries who came to Jerusalem after three centuries of Ottoman rule created new churches from among Orthodox members who converted to Western Christian denominations. This is a wound to the Orthodox churches up to this day.

All this helps explain the problems related to the holy places—mistrust belies ecumenical cooperation. There have also been problems related to proselytism by the missionary churches, and there is fear among the Greek Orthodox that theological dialogue will be used to argue that there are no real differences among the churches. Still, important progress has been made since the 1950s. Restoration has necessitated interfaith cooperation, lest everything fall down. The completion of the dome over the Holy Sepulchre was celebrated by patriarchs of the Greek Orthodox church.

The intifada forced the Christian churches to work together on issues of justice and peace. A common memorandum on the significance of Jerusalem for the Christian churches was signed by all the main churches in 1994. Mixed marriages have contributed to ecumenical openness, and most laypeople spontaneously describe themselves as Christian, whereas clergy use more specific denominational reference points. Coming up with a common date for the celebrations of Christmas and Easter is seen as desirable, but the question of a just and durable peace is the most important issue.

The Old City of Jerusalem is divided into Arab, Jewish, Christian, and Armenian sections, and the entire area is enclosed within high stone walls. The Jewish section has been rebuilt and resembles a renovated section of an old American city, like Ghirardelli Square in San Francisco, with wide walkways and well-lit, spacious shops. The other three sections are crowded with humanity and full of smells, sounds, and an exotic feel. The walkways wind around and intersect like a maze, so it's hard to maintain a sense of direction. Shopkeepers offer bargains in circus-barker English.

I visited three key sites within the Old City: the Church of the Holy Sepulchre (the traditional place of Christ's burial), the Wailing Wall (the Jewish access point to one wall of the Temple), and the Dome of the Rock mosque (where Muhammad is said to have ascended into heaven). Holy Sepulchre is a dark, rather somber church that is divided up among the different Christian denominations. Except for personal piety connected to the historical features of Calvary and the presence of the tomb that Joseph of Arimathea made available for Jesus' burial, it is not a particularly edifying place. I arrived at a good time to enter the tomb area because the line was short. In one of the nearby chapels, a group of Japanese Catholic pilgrims was celebrating Mass.

The Wailing Wall is next to a great open space with heavy security; one must go through a police checkpoint to gain entry. The prayer site in front of the wall has an ablution area for ritual purification, and then a fence perpendicular to the wall; men pray on the left side of the fence, women on the right. The men wear the yarmulke as a sign of God's presence. On the day I visited, about a quarter of the men wore traditional Hasidic dress—black pants, coats, and wide-brimmed hats. Most had beards, long hair locks on the sides, and belts with tassels hanging down.

Looming above the Wailing Wall are the sacred places for Muslims, a proximity that has triggered violent conflicts through the years. The El-Aqsa Mosque was burned by a Jewish terrorist but has been renovated. Across an open square from El-Aqsa is the Dome of the Rock Mosque, where guests are made welcome after taking off their shoes and paying an entry fee.

Several fundamentalist Christian groups believe that Israel must be in control of all its ancient territories before the Second Coming of the Messiah and the Final Judgment. For this reason they are strong American supporters of an aggressive Israeli military stance in the West Bank. The irony is that they are only short-term allies, because they believe all those who reject the Messiah when he comes will be damned.

I am in favor of peace with justice in the Middle East. How to achieve it beyond prayers and hard work is the mystery.

Of all the places I have visited in my life, Masada—the Herodian fortress overlooking the Dead Sea, and the last holdout place of the radical Jews who resisted Roman rule—ranks in my top five. It is ancient, dramatic, historically significant, and well preserved. Because of its isolated setting, with a little imagination you can feel yourself back in another millennium. It is located on a flat peak atop an isolated mountain on the eastern slopes of the Judean desert, 440 meters above the sea. The topography of Masada, its remoteness, its natural fortifications, and its isolation made it a perfect location for a fortress during the Second Temple period.

Herod, who ruled under Roman patronage, chose Masada as a place of refuge from his enemies, building fortifications and splendid palaces on the mountaintop. In A.D. 66, at the beginning of the Great Revolt against Rome, a group of Sicarii commanded by Menahem Ben-Yehuda of Galilee captured Masada from the Roman garrison, and it became a refuge during the years of the revolt. After the destruction of the Temple in A.D. 70, the last rebels reached Masada.

Two years later the Roman army attacked the fortress with a force of 10,000 to 15,000 men. The occupants of Masada numbered 967 men, women, and children. The siege lasted several months, and as the Romans prepared to complete their conquest, the inhabitants of Masada decided to take their own lives rather than be captured. In an orderly way, they killed one another in groups, and the last one alive set fire to the wooden buildings and threw himself on his sword. Thus the fortress was delivered into Roman hands. Today, members of the Israeli military take an oath atop the fortress at night: "Never again will Masada fall."

Qumran, not far from Masada, was the home of the

Essenes, a breakaway sect of Judaism for two centuries up until the defeat at Masada. In 1947, Bedouin shepherds happened upon seven ancient scrolls in a cave, and additional scrolls were discovered between 1951 and 1956. Hidden in jars for nearly two thousand years and preserved by the area's arid climate, the scrolls included books of the Old Testament, the Apocrypha, and the sect's own works. The Essenes were ascetics who paid a great deal of attention to ritual bathing and purity and who lived a common life in a settlement that was constructed to make them as self-reliant as possible, with assembly halls, a central dining room for ceremonial meals, a kitchen, ritual baths, a laundry room, a watchtower, a stable, and a pottery workshop. Two Notre Dame professors, Gene Ulrich and Jim VanderKam, have been involved in translating and commenting on the scrolls.

In the spring of 2000, an international conference on a Christological theme at Tantur brought me to Israel once again, and I took advantage of the visit to spend a week touring the Holy Land with my sister and brother-in-law, Mary and John Long. Before I left home, the Middle East had been constantly in the news. There was violence in the West Bank, violence in southern Lebanon, and an abrupt withdrawal of all Israeli troops (and many of their collaborators) from Lebanon. Yet on our drive from the Tel Aviv airport to Tantur, you would have thought we were in a quiet part of the States. Traffic moved along freely, and there was no sign of military presence except for the planes and helicopters sitting at one end of the airport.

A pilgrimage to the Holy Land is a kind of reversal in which, from the vantage point of two thousand years after the time of Jesus, we return to the land of his origins to experience the scandal of particularity. We seek the Jesus of history, who is no longer visible, so that we might draw the connection between what he said and did: his teachings, his miraculous healings, his courage in the face of hostility.

We began our tour in Jerusalem, driving past the Temple Mount, the Jewish cemetery, and the Garden of Gethsemane, and on through Abu Dis, an Arab town recently given back to the Palestinian authorities. Once you clear Jerusalem proper on the road to Jericho, you pass Bedouin encampments with camels, tents, and a variety of animals. You also see dramatic Jewish settlements created in the middle of some of the harshest climate anywhere. All this is West Bank territory that has not been returned to Palestinian control.

In Jericho we stopped at a sycamore tree said to be two thousand years old and connected to the story of Zacchaeus and Jesus. From there we drove to the hill beneath the Monastery of the Temptation, a forbidding place carved out of stone on the side of a mountain, where we had tea and coffee with a Bedouin family who were friends of our driver. A cable car now climbs from the ruins of ancient Jericho to the monastery.

The Jordan River is not very wide until you get closer to Galilee, but the presence of the river has been immense in human history. Its water makes possible the settlement that now flourishes there. The wide valley is lush and green, nourishing every kind of fruit, melon, and vegetables— dates and figs, watermelons and sunflowers, corn, bananas, and mangoes. There are even crocodile farms maintained for pelts.

We stopped near where the Sea of Galilee empties into the Jordan River, a site that is popular with evangelical Protestants who want to be rebaptized in the Jordan. We watched several people go through that ritual, including a group clad in white robes who were totally immersed. Few boats are allowed on the Sea of Galilee, so there is a sense of its beauty having been preserved. At lunch in a waterside restaurant north of Tiberias, I had Saint Peter's Fish, believed to have been the fish Peter caught when Christ told him to cast out his nets in the Sea of Galilee.

At Capernaum we visited a famous archeological excavation where various Christian churches were built adjacent to Peter's home. Next we drove to the Church of the Multiplication of the Loaves and Fishes, a prayerful spot, and then to the Church of the Primacy of Saint Peter. Finally, we drove up to the Monastery of the Beatitudes, where a few months earlier Pope John Paul II had gathered with hundreds of thousands of young people from all over the world. The setting, with its quiet, colorful gardens and beautiful chapel looking out over the Sea of Galilee, is one of the most moving and religiously inspiring spots in all the world. This was where Jesus preached to the crowds and gathered his disciples. The message of the Sermon on the Mount continues to attract believers with its challenges and its consolations. This spot's mix of historical reliability, sheer natural beauty, and profound impact on human history restores the spirit of visitors from around the world.

The next day we toured the Golan Heights. Israel has no natural claim to this land except for military considerations. (High ground is always valuable, and the highest peaks of the Golan are full of Israeli observation and listening posts.) The road we took was the scene of intense fighting during the so called Six-Day War in 1967. Israeli tank superiority carried the day, and a number of Syrian towns were destroyed, some of them visible on our trip. We passed various tank bases and saw signs on both sides of the highway warning of mines in the fields. The farthest I had gone previously in this area was to the overlook of the destroyed town of Kuneitra, but this time we kept going and passed through the Druse towns of Mas'ada and Majdal Shams. (The Druse are a Muslim sect with their own distinctive beliefs and way of dress; the men wear a certain type of white turban.)

We visited Nimrod Fortress, near the point where Syria, Israel, and Lebanon converge. The fortress is now a national park on the slopes of Mount Hermon at an altitude of 2,675 feet above sea level, making it the highest peak in the Middle East. In winter it is snow-capped, and even in June areas of snow were visible. This is the source of much of the water that becomes the River Jordan. Nimrod Fortress is one of the largest and most impressive Middle East fortresses to have survived from the Middle Ages. It controlled the road that ran from Tyre on the Mediterranean to Damascus and was virtually impregnable.

From the fortress we proceeded down to Nabal Hermon, alias Banias or Caesarea Philippi. This marks the headwaters of the Jordan, where water comes rushing out of the mountains and forms a beautiful waterfall. In the area are caves where an ancient temple to the god Ram and a later temple to one of the Roman emperors were located. Nine kilometers away, two smaller rivers join up and become the Jordan River before it swells into the Sea of Galilee. Matthew 16:13 says it was at Caesarea Philippi that Peter proclaimed his faith in Jesus and received the keys of the kingdom.

Next we drove to Metulla, a border city with Lebanon on the very northernmost tip of Israel. An Israeli military guard stopped us right before the border crossing. Two weeks earlier, this area was full of gun battles as the Israeli army withdrew from a ten-mile strip of Lebanon. We had a clear view into Lebanon, including a military fort that the Israelis destroyed before they left. From Metulla we drove to Qiryat Shemona, a major Israeli settlement city that is frequently in the news when Lebanese guerrillas shell Israel. Two weeks earlier, violent attacks were taking place there, and air-raid shelters are a way of life. Otherwise, it is a rich agricultural area.

The next day we were off to Cana and Nazareth. Cana is a decent-size town with a church at the reputed site of the miracle at the wedding feast. The church and the town did not do much for us. Nazareth was a different story. It's an all-Arab city that used to be equally split between Muslim and Christian, but the decline in the number of Christians (mainly through emigration) raises doubts about the continuing presence of Christian believers and worshipers in the Holy Land. The Church of the Annunciation is modern in style but tasteful and beautiful. Within the church courtyard but outside the church itself are various depictions of Mary and the Baby Jesus as viewed by different national cultures. The basilica was completed in 1969, and many groups of pilgrims, including an English-speaking group, were having Mass when we were there.

From Nazareth we drove to Mount Tabor, the site of the Transfiguration. Mount Tabor is a high peak with a switchback road to the top. Some Jews were parasailing from near the top, and the prevailing winds pulled them high above us. At the top of Tabor there is a plain and simple Romanesque church.

Proceeding south, we passed into Palestinian territory in the West Bank, where the settlements in the nonagricultural Jewish communities tend to be gleaming-white buildings on the tops of hills and mountains, while the Arab villages tend to be no more than two-thirds of the way up the hills, or else in the lowlands. The Israeli settlements provide cheap, subsidized housing, which is part of the right-wing Israeli claim that all this territory is part of the Promised Land even if the population is predominantly Arab.

We drove to Sebaste (Samaria), a significant city in Old Testament times as well as in the Roman era, and from there through Nablus and Ramallah. Both cities appear on American television periodically when there are confrontations between teenagers and Israeli soldiers. Nablus has steep hills on both sides, with a lot of apartment developments, and is the largest city in the West Bank. Ramallah is only about fifteen miles from Jerusalem, so it is like a far suburb; one end has refugee camps near Jewish settlers, with troops between them. The side of Ramallah nearest to Jerusalem has many lovely houses and mansions owned by Palestinians, some from the States. About half the houses in the West Bank have concrete and girders in place to add another story or an extension when the money to do so becomes available. I guess that is a sign of hope for what tomorrow might bring.

The twentieth-century Church of Mary, Ark of the Covenant at Abu Ghosh, a few miles west of Jerusalem, affords a sweeping view in three directions, although the church itself is rather plain. The site has religious significance that goes back to worship of Baal, the ultimate pagan deity. The Ark of the Covenant was said to be kept there until it was captured by the Philistines. Now Mary is honored under one of her traditional titles.

At Yad Vashem, the Holocaust museum where Pope John Paul II issued his apology for the events of the Holocaust, a display recounts the evolution of anti-Jewish ideology under the Nazis, concluding in the mass killings in the concentration camps. The power of the display is largely carried by the photographs and the staggering statistics. The Holocaust museum in Washington, D.C., has more artifacts, however, and after visiting Auschwitz-Birkenau in Poland, I doubt that anything else would be as shocking. Among the crowds of visitors at Yad Vashem were Israeli military recruits toting their rifles.

From Yad Vashem we went to Ein Karem, where we visited the Church of John the Baptist, on the reputed site of his birth, and the Church of the Visitation, on the site of Mary's visit with her cousin, Elizabeth, when both were with child. The Franciscans oversee both churches, as they do many others in the Holy Land. (I grew up with frequent visits to the Franciscan-run Shrine of the Holy Land in my neighborhood in D.C.) I have to wonder how attractive such a mission is today, when the Christian community in the Holy Land is so diminished. In a sense, the Franciscans keep these sacred sites available for Christian pilgrims.

From Ein Karem we paid a brief visit to the Chagall Windows at the synagogue of the Hadassah-Hebrew University Medical Center. They represent the twelve sons of the patriarch Jacob, the forefather of the twelve tribes of Israel. Prominent are floating figures of animals, fish, flowers, and numerous Jewish symbols. Then we drove to a modern American-style Jewish mall, one sign of the affluence of Jewish society. Security was tight, because such places are prime targets for terrorists.

Next, our travels took us in the direction of Beersheba, one of the great caravan cities of the past. The closer you get to Beersheba, the more common become the Bedouin encampments. Some still maintain a nomadic-shepherd lifestyle, and we saw many camels and sheep and goats. You wonder what they think when they watch American soaps or quiz shows. Closer to the big city were more-elaborate houses and other accoutrements of civilization such as satellite dishes. Beersheba is a fairly large city but is primarily mainstream Israeli.

Tel Arad, in Israeli territory just south of the West Bank, is a major archeological site where the earliest evidence of human presence goes back six thousand years. Today it consists of the ruins of a Canaanite city (third millennium B.C.) and fortresses built by the kings of Judea dating to the Israelite period. Arad is mentioned in the Bible as one of the cities in the eastern Negev whose inhabitants prevented the Israelites from entering the Promised Land, and the King of Arad appears in the list of Canaanite kings vanquished by Joshua during the conquest of the land of Israel.

From Tel Arad we drove to Hebron, the burial place of Abraham, Isaac, and Jacob, the three great patriarchs, and their wives. It is sacred to both Jews and Muslims, and a synagogue and mosque sit side by side there. A number of years ago, a demented Jewish settler massacred twenty or thirty Muslims in Hebron and set off widespread rioting.

Spending concentrated time touring with my sister and brother-in-law was a blessing. We saw no overt violence, although we did visit some places where there had been violence recently. Yet for most people most of the time, it was much safer to be there than in the majority of American cities.

Everything about the Israeli–Palestinian question is complex and deeply textured. History, ancient and modern, is the prism through which various claims to the land and to sovereignty are made. As in Northern Ireland, while the religious roles of the various sides are clear, it is not self-evident that religion is the driving force. The

Israelis have done to the land what the Mormons did to Utah: transformed it and made it fertile. The main difference is that, for the experiment to work here, others had to be kicked out.

I always find my time in the Holy Land to be a real pilgrimage. It is where the Word became incarnate. It is where God's human face shone forth. It is the land of Jesus and Mary and Joseph, of all their Jewish forebearers, and of the early Christian community. For Christians and Jews and Muslims, it is the land of our origins in faith, the fount from which we can continue to know meaning and inspiration. It was a privilege to return there.

ROME

My travels have taken me to Rome nearly a dozen times. Each visit had a particular purpose, but underlying them all has been my desire to make Notre Dame well known in Vatican circles, and I believe the visits accomplished that.

The Vatican has many levels. It is a spiritual and pilgrimage site. It is the center of the Church's bureaucracy. It is a tourist center and a financial engine. It is the home base of the Pope. The Vatican has a wide range of people working within it, ranging from selfless, committed servants of the faith to arrogant, ambitious careerists and everything in between. As in all centers of power, rumor and gossip abound. I must admit that, other than the fundamental sense of loyalty I feel as a Roman Catholic and a priest, I am not attracted to the Vatican scene. Much of the pomp and formalism I find off-putting, and I am hardly unique in these feelings. For many American religious, especially those with advanced degrees, service in the Curia is an unattractive career path. For many diocesan clergy, on the other hand, it is a route toward upward mobility and influence.

I realize that every organization needs a central bureaucracy, but the ponderous and tradition-laden folkways of the Vatican are a reality that every Pope must deal with from day one, just as every national leader must. Who are the trusted advisers? Who controls access? Who offers rewards for a job well done, and of what kind? Titles are extremely important, for they determine one's place in the pecking order. For clerics, the progression is priest, monsignor, bishop, archbishop, cardinal, perhaps even Pope. Career bureaucrats work their way up, sometimes very slowly. One prized benefit is access to Vatican housing, especially near one's office.

I have found in my dealings in Rome that most administrators clothe themselves in the mantle of the Pope to enhance their own authority. This can be employed for good ends or for Machiavellian trickery and self-aggrandizement. Because all the top jobs are held by celibate men, the temptation is for one's work to become one's whole life. In choosing to honor the heads of various Roman congregations with honorary degrees at Notre Dame, we have tried to choose Curia leaders who have the best reputations as pastors and effective ministers of the Gospel.

I personally like many of the people I have met on my

visits to Rome; they seem dedicated to the good of the Church and are men of prayer. Yet I wish that the broader church community would have more of an impact on the Vatican as a bureaucracy, and I wish more of those chosen for jobs at the Vatican had spent more time away from Rome, in the local church more than in the diplomatic corps. I also wish there were more women and married people entrusted with major leadership responsibility.

Saint Peter's is an amazing building. It is the largest church in the world and huge in every dimension, yet every aspect is in such perfect scale that it seems quite intimate. The sacristy in Saint Peter's is a beehive in the mornings, when many of the Vatican priests or bishop-bureaucrats, as well as priests with tour groups from around the world, arrive to offer Mass. Fortunately, there are altars all around the main floor of Saint Peter's as well as in the crypt. One Mass I celebrated in Saint Peter's was in the crypt at the Lithuanian chapel, right around the corner from Saint Peter's tomb. It was a thrill to celebrate Mass in a location that goes back to the first Christians.

Although it's true that the evidence of Saint Peter actually being buried there has been contested, I believe that archeologists have made the case convincingly. The high altar of Saint Peter's is directly over that subterranean site. The first reading from Ephesians on the feast of Saint Thomas the Apostle says, "You are part of a building that has the apostles and prophets for its foundations, and Christ Jesus himself for its main cornerstone." In a sense, all of Christianity has its origin in this claim.

In the basement of Saint Peter's, where the tombs of recent popes are located, a number of people can always be found praying before Pope John XXIII's remains, which are displayed in an open casket. The remains are said to be preserved, although I found it hard to tell from a quick perusal in a fast-moving line of viewers. Even though Pope John is one of my Church heroes, I am indifferent to claims about bodily integrity. It is not part of my piety, as it goes against Christian notions of the meaning of the resurrection from the dead.

Walking around Old Rome is always an adventure for me, because none of the streets runs straight and the curves in the Tiber River make it difficult to figure out where in the heck you are at a given moment. In the area around the Vatican there is always a combination of tourists, pilgrims, workers, hawkers, clerics and religious, police, guides, onlookers, cabbies, beggars, bus drivers, and the whole retinue of people that sustain one of the great religious centers of the world. Buses disgorge streams of visitors, and vendors try to sell them kitsch papal images and anything with the papal seal or colors. Depending on how you view it, the whole thing can inspire, befuddle, depress, or enchant; in my visits I have experienced all those feelings and more.

When you are dressed in clerical garb on the streets of Rome, you get vibes that the general populace is still fairly anticlerical. Some Roman men cover their genitals with both hands when clerics walk by, lest they become sterile. It makes me want to zap them to see if it works. Perhaps these attitudes are to be expected in a city with such an overwhelming presence of the institutional Church.

The catacombs surrounding Rome contain the remains of more than half a million Christians who were buried there in the early centuries, when Christianity was illegal in Rome. Saint Callixtus is the largest and most revered of the catacombs because it was the burial place of nine popes and eight bishops of the third century. In times of persecution, the catacombs were not only places of burial but also places where the Eucharist could be celebrated clandestinely on top of the bones of the martyrs.

SPAIN

In four visits to Spain and three to Portugal, I've managed to see a fair portion of both countries. Two of my Spanish visits took me to Madrid, a grand capital of broad boulevards and countless parks whose public monuments and buildings reminded me of Paris, Rome, and London. Bullfighting, while generally scorned internationally, is still a big part of Spanish culture. It combines tradition, ritual, spectacle, and danger; three or four toreadors a year are killed, and many others are wounded. Overall, that is a better record than car racing or skyjumping, not to speak of high-peak mountain climbing.

The Escorial monastery, about twenty-seven miles northwest of Madrid, is where most of Spain's royalty are buried. Escorial has the status of our Mount Vernon or the White House as a place for all Spanish children and families to visit. During one of my visits I managed to look into the main church just as the museum and crypt were closing. To my surprise, I saw the Mormon Tabernacle Choir, in red dresses and black tuxes, rehearsing for a concert. I could only guess what earlier Spanish authorities might have thought of this ecumenical openness.

Toledo, the former capital of Spain and one of the country's great cities, is the site of Notre Dame's undergraduate program in Spain. The students study at the José Ortega y Gasset Foundation, taking courses designed specifically for students from the United States, Japan, and Latin America.

The Synagogue de Transito is one of two remaining synagogues in Toledo. The treatment of the Jews by various Spanish governments, especially during the time of the Inquisition, is a blot on the national history. The choices were conversion, exile, or death.

Seville is considered the fun-loving part of Spain and the home of flamenco dancing and fragrant flowers. Its cathedral is the world's third largest, after Saint Peter's in Rome and Saint Paul's in London. It contains a tomb for Christopher Columbus, who was originally buried in what is now the Dominican Republic.

The Church in Spain has gone through a difficult transition since the death of Francisco Franco. It was closely aligned with his dictatorial regime and the Old Order, but as Spain opened up under democracy, the influence of media, travel, and trade called the past into question.

Since World War II, Spain, Ireland, and Poland have been the most active centers of Catholicism in Europe, and Catholic Christianity is deeply embedded in Spain's culture and sense of identity. Yet religious practice among the young has declined, as have the number of religious and clerical vocations.

One facet of the Church in Spain is Opus Dei ("the work of God"), which was founded in the twentieth century by a Spanish priest as an organization primarily for lay Catholics, though it now has many bishops in the hierarchies of Spain and Latin America. Although critics decry the organization's secretiveness, rigid spirituality, and hostile critique of post–Vatican II Catholicism, Opus Dei has been favored by Pope John Paul II, who made it a prelature and appointed a number of members to Vatican bureaucratic positions. My own experience leads me to be basically unfavorable toward the movement.

Santiago de Compostela, located in a relatively isolated area in the far northwest corner of Spain, was one of the great pilgrimage centers of the world in the Middle Ages, comparable to Canterbury, Rome, and the Holy Land, thanks to an early ninth-century bishop who decided that the tomb of the apostle James, son of Zebedee, or Santiago the Elder, was in the area. Medieval tales described James as preaching in the region, and after he was beheaded in Jerusalem his body was said to have been spirited away by disciples and brought to Spain. So many pilgrims have placed their hands on a stone column in the cathedral's front entrance that a smooth spot in the shape of a hand is worn into the stone.

Some pilgrims are also said to bang their heads three times on the column to induce clarity of thought. I tried the hand part but not the head banging.

One unique thing about the basilica is an ancient, giant thurible, or incense device, which is connected to ropes that stretch to the ceiling and move on a pulley. On Sundays and special occasions, six men come out after Communion and manipulate the rope so that the incenser swoops at 50 miles an hour across the area in front of the altar. At the top of its arc, it almost touches the 180-foot-high ceiling. It is one of the most extraordinary liturgical displays I've ever seen. As the incenser moved to the peak of its arc, fire and smoke were clearly visible within. In order not to be in the line of flight, I moved a bit.

Spain has changed tremendously since the Franco years, both economically and in terms of the roles played by the police and the army. The country is more European than it once was, but also more regional, with a decentralized government and a resurgence of special language and cultural groupings. The change in the relative position of women has been dramatic, with many more now in positions of real responsibility. Contemporary Spaniards work hard, and the days of the long siesta are past.

PORTUGAL

Fatima, located almost straight north of Lisbon, is one of the great Marian shrines of the world. The story of Fatima is simple: Between May 13 and October 13, 1917, Mary appeared six times to three shepherd children. It was during World War I, when Portugal was controlled by an anticlerical government, and the heart of Mary's message was prayer, penance, and consecration. That was also the year of the Russian Revolution, and some of her message was connected to the role that Russia would play in the world.

She stressed praying the rosary daily, wearing the brown scapular, and performing acts of reparation and sacrifice, and her message requested that Russia be consecrated to the Immaculate Heart of Mary. Three "secrets" were said to be entrusted to the children: the first was a vision of hell, the second was the prediction of World War II, and the third was not to be disclosed except to the Pope. It became the source of endless speculation.

Although the Catholic Church makes no definitive claims for the authenticity of any particular Marian apparition, certain ones have some acceptance both in popular piety and with the hierarchical church. Although these messages can never replace the Gospel, the centrality of Jesus, or the apostolic witness, Christians across the ages have found consolation and strength in their faith through Marian devotion. It is by the fruits of such phenomena that they are tested, and while Marian devotion admits of excess, distortion, and false prophecy, like all popular religion the simplicity of the message and the lay adaptability of the prayer practices have often found ready responsiveness.

I come from a family where Mary has an honored place. My mother left her crutches behind at the Shrine of

Our Lady of Victory when she was a girl and has recited the rosary and the novena of Our Lady of Victory every day since. My father also had a deep devotion to Mary. I participate in a university named after Mary, where her image in gold atop a dome represents us all, and where the Grotto of Our Lady of Lourdes has been a center of prayer and favor to multiple generations. I often claim that Notre Dame has become a center of pilgrimage, so my own pilgrimage to Fatima was fitting.

The town of Fatima is dominated by the shrine and the pilgrims who visit it—about four million a year. The name "Fatima" may derive from the daughter of the prophet Muhammad, a vestige from the era of Moorish influence. The shrine's esplanade, which is bigger than Saint Peter's Square, can hold a million people, but the church is no bigger than the main part of Sacred Heart Basilica on Notre Dame's campus. Images on the walls represent the fifteen mysteries of the rosary, and high above the altar is a painting of Mary. On either side of the altar are the tombs of the two children who have died.

During my visit, I offered Mass at an outdoor covered altar. I also went to the fields where the apparitions took place and visited the home of the girl Lucy.

EASTERN EUROPE

RUSSIA

In the summer of 1999 I took a trip to Russia as part of a Notre Dame group that was visiting Saint Petersburg. That city, called Leningrad during the Communist era, was the capital of Russia in the days of the Empire and became the center of the Russian Revolution in 1917. Hitler laid siege to it in 1941, thinking he could crush the Russian spirit if he captured the city named after Lenin. He was wrong. (In an earlier era, Napoleon made the same mistake.) Although Leningrad's food supply was cut off by a 900-day German siege and the winter of 1941–42 was terribly cold, Hitler failed to take the city, and that failure marked the beginning of the end of Germany's Eastern Front. In 1991, by a popular vote, the name of the city was changed back to Saint Petersburg.

As the main celebrant at a Mass one evening, I called to mind all those years when we used to pray at the end of Mass for the conversion of Russia. What a transformation we have seen in our lifetime! It is one of the greatest achievements of Pope John Paul II that he played such a crucial role in this process.

Who would have thought I'd spend a Fourth of July on a peaceful day in Russia, the "evil empire"? For two and a half hours that day we toured the Hermitage Museum, which has one of the world's great collections of Western art and is so large that it's said if you spent one minute in front of each display, it would take ten years to see the entire museum. On our way back to our hotel, a traffic policemen stopped our van, but after checking the driver's

papers he let us go. I would hate to write a letter from the
"Saint Petersburg jail."

I concluded that Russians are the prototypical
Caucasian people in terms of physical appearance: they
are white—not pink or tan or beige or some other off-white
shade—but white in a kind of pure sense, like the people
in parts of Africa are black in a pure sense. Since the word
"Caucasian" comes from the Caucasus Mountains, I guess
that makes sense. Also, Russians don't smile a lot.
Historically they have had a lot of reasons not to.

As a tourist site, Saint Petersburg is one of the great
wonders of the world. You could spend weeks visiting all
the worthwhile places. Let's hope Russia eventually gets a
decent government and a chance to develop as a free,
prosperous society. Maybe then people can smile again.

POLAND

For one hundred years, from about 1817 to 1917, Poland
ceased to exist as an independent nation, but the Polish
language and the Roman Catholic religion have been the
country's glue in times of adversity. Pope John Paul II is a
national hero; his multicity trip to Poland not long before
my visit brought out millions of people. After all the suf-
fering the Polish people have endured in the twentieth
century, it must be nice to have one of their own in such a
prominent position.

Wadowice is the site of the Pope's three-bedroom
boyhood home and of the church where he was baptized.

The home now contains a modest but interesting display that covers the equivalent of six rooms (twice what his family occupied) and includes artifacts, photographs, and family materials.

From Wadowice I went to Auschwitz. I have studied quite a bit about Nazi Germany, about anti-Semitism, and about the ideological underpinnings that unleashed such horror on the world. I have also seen *Schindler's List*, *Europa Europa*, *Sophie's Choice*, and other movies that deal with the Holocaust, and I've read much of Elie Wiesel and other novelists who portray their own and others' experience of survival. But there is nothing like being there. A tour of Auschwitz is realistic, heart-wrenching, macabre, and imaginatively engaging all at the same time. There are pictures of the prisoners and displays of hair, eyeglasses, luggage, crockery, and so on; drawings depicting the daily round of activities; and preserved cell areas where the crowding was animal-like. You see the poisoning rooms, the ovens, the barbed-wire fences, and the guard towers. Perhaps it is the pictures of the children that are most disturbing.

Auschwitz/Birkenau was a highly refined system for killing as many people as possible as quickly as possible. The total was around 1.5 million by the end of the war. Of these, about 900,000 were Jews and the rest were Polish political prisoners, priests, gypsies, homosexuals, and Russian soldiers. At first, Auschwitz prisoners were shot or hanged; later, the Nazis experimented with poison gas, which was efficient and lethal. Eventually whole sections of Auschwitz were set aside for massive gassings and the burning of the bodies. Finally Birkenau was created as an assembly line for killing by gas.

As the prison trains pulled in from all over Europe, army doctors divided up the prisoners. Those of potential usefulness were shunted to Auschwitz; everyone else went to Birkenau for a sure death sentence. Some women were set aside to serve as prostitutes. Even at Auschwitz, few survived more than three months. Prisoners who were given enforcement authority in the camps (called "capos") enjoyed special privileges, but they were eventually killed too. Horrible medical experimentation went on in the camps, even with children. Birkenau today is like a state fairground with a few brick and wooden structures preserved, but otherwise endless rows of chimneys where the bodies were burned.

I guess the best reaction to that whole scene is not despair at what the human race is capable of, but rather hope that we can learn from the past. Our guide told us that after some visitors from South Africa were shown the two camps, they asked her if she believed all this had really happened. They clearly did not. This is part of the challenge of keeping this story alive.

My next stop was Czestochowa, the site of the Marian shrine known as Jasna Gora, with its famous icon of the Black Madonna. Jasna Gora is the religious, cultural, and national center of Poland and the second-most visited Marian shrine in Europe, after Lourdes. The holy icon of the Black Madonna is considered the sacred emblem of

Poland, akin to Our Lady of Guadalupe in Latin America. The face of Mary is the focus of attention on the icon, and she holds Jesus in her arms. Other than the faces and the hands, the rest of the icon wears clothes of gold, silver, and other colors, which are changed periodically. Pope John Paul has had a close relationship to the shrine, both in his younger years and since he became Pope. On his last visit there, a million people were present.

Poland is probably the most Catholic country in the world at present, and I was impressed by the manifest piety of the pilgrims of all ages at Jasna Gora. There were youth groups that had come by bike, and families making the Stations of the Cross, praying the rosary, and going to confession. Long-standing traditions were being enacted as though they were the most natural things in the world.

I also spent some time in Warsaw at the remnants of the city's Ghetto, where the Jews revolted against the Nazis in 1943. Most of the Ghetto residents were eventually sent to Treblinka, the closest concentration camp. The rebels never had a chance militarily, and they knew it, but the revolt was a statement about human dignity and resistance to evil. In the middle of the Ghetto area today there is a park with a sculpture honoring the leaders of the uprising. As in the rest of the city, very few of the original buildings were spared, but there are marble slabs around the perimeter as a reminder.

There are also heroic sculptures depicting the Warsaw Uprising in 1944, a citywide effort to resist the Nazis as their war machine began to collapse. The tragic result was the death of a quarter of a million Poles and the near obliteration of the physical face of Warsaw. Some residents survived by escaping through the sewer system, and some of the city's historical artifacts were taken into the countryside and hidden.

The Poles, like the Czechs and the Hungarians, have a pervasive and deep-seated hatred for the Germans and the Russians. Of a prewar population of 1.3 million, only 500,000 people in Warsaw survived World War II. Nationally, 6 million Poles were killed in that war, including 4 million Jews. In 1940 Stalin ordered the secret police to shoot more than four thousand Polish military officers who had been taken prisoner when the Soviet Union invaded Poland and to bury them in the Katyn Forest. The Soviets then blamed the Nazis, a fiction that continued until 1990. Memories of similar events haunt the Polish consciousness.

HUNGARY

The basilica in Esztergom is one of the most beautiful churches I have seen. In a deep crypt is the burial place of all the bishops of Hungarian history, and one section has the remains of Cardinal Jozsef Mindszenty, who resisted the Communists in the late 1940s and was charged with treason and imprisoned. Mindszenty was a symbol of resistance that I remember from my youth. After the 1956 revolution, he was given refuge in the American Embassy, and when his health failed he was spirited to Austria, where he died. But he had pledged that he would return to

Hungary after the Russians left, so when they were finally gone his remains were carried in procession across Hungary to Esztergom, accompanied by more than one hundred thousand people. His tomb is now a place of pilgrimage for many people, including Pope John Paul II.

The Communists imprisoned hundreds of priests and nuns after 1945, with the goal of wiping out all vestiges of religion within twenty years. Gradually some accommodation was achieved, but the secret police kept tabs on those who practiced their religion, and careers and reputations were on the line. For almost fifty years Catholics received minimal religious instruction, and even the sacraments—baptisms, weddings, funerals—required clandestine arrangements. A post-Soviet concordat with the Vatican pledged a gradual return of seized property back to the church.

One of Hungary's heroes is Saint Stephen, the country's first king, who was crowned on Christmas Day in A.D. 1000 and converted the pagan Magyars to Christianity. His clenched right hand is the country's most highly revered relic. A more recent hero is Imre Nagy, the prime minister executed after the 1956 revolution. In Hungary, dislike of the Russians is pervasive today, and when I was there only one monument that made any reference to the Russians remained in the country.

LATIN AMERICA

EL SALVADOR

In the 1980s and early 1990s, El Salvador went through a horrible civil war that reflected the Cold War and the ideological feuds of that period. In 1980, Archbishop Oscar Romero was shot through the heart during the offertory part of the Mass by soldiers in a car outside, and soon after that four American churchwomen were raped and murdered along a highway. A few years later, five Jesuits and two housekeepers were murdered at their residence at the University of Central America.

During a visit I paid to the country in 2003, I went to the church where Archbishop Romero was murdered. By the time I found it, the church was unlit and no one was around, but a nun was persuaded to let me in. On the wall of one of the rooms where Romero lived were dramatic pictures taken right after he was shot: nuns were holding up his head, and blood was flowing from his mouth and nose, but he was clearly already dead. You could see the sense of panic and dismay on the faces of those present. Adjoined to the pictures was a cabinet with a number of his garments and personal effects, including the blood-soaked vestments that he was wearing for the Mass. Right outside the house, someone had produced a bright, colorful mural picturing Romero in his prime.

During an earlier trip to El Salvador, I visited the University of Central America, where the six Jesuit priests and two housekeepers had been murdered. I viewed the site of the murders with Jon Sobrino, S.J., one of the better-known liberation theologians, who was a member of the local Jesuit community when the killings took place. He happened to be out of the country then, and thus was spared death.

The prelude to the murders occurred some days before, when the army stopped at the Jesuit residence looking for Father Ignacio Ellacuria, who was high on their wanted list. On the fateful day, a large group of soldiers entered the property, grabbed five Jesuits from their rooms, took them to the back garden, and shot them. A sixth Jesuit, who was sleeping but heard the commotion, was killed when he went outside. Finally, the soldiers killed two housekeepers before shooting randomly to make it look like there had been a shootout. For some reason, they tried to put one of the bodies in Father Sobrino's room. The priest later told me only one book fell from his bookshelf that day: Jürgen Moltmann's *The Crucified God.*

On the site there now is a deeply moving memorial to the martyrs: six red rose bushes for the Jesuits and a yellow rose bush in the middle for the two housekeepers. A nearby shrine honors not only this group but also Archbishop Romero and the eleven other priests and four American women religious who were killed during the war. The two major feast days in El Salvador now are March 24, the day when Romero was killed, and November 16, in memory of the Jesuit slayings.

For anyone interested in these events, I recommend three movies: *Roses in December*, about the killing of the American religious women by the army; *Romero*, about the life and death of the Archbishop; and *Salvador*, about the conflict in that country. There were atrocities on all sides of the civil war, but my visit was a graphic reminder of why reconciliation at the national level is so difficult to achieve.

In 1999 I discussed the issue of postwar reconciliation with President José Maria Tojeira, S.J., president of the University of Central America. He was the provincial when the Jesuits were killed, and he told me that while he had no problem forgiving those who committed or ordered the crimes, he could not accept a form of reconciliation that honored the killers and did not respect the peasants. He wanted a proper focus on the events of the war.

The university, he said, was proposing a four-stage process of reconciliation: (1) revealing the truth, (2) seeking justice for all parties, (3) implementing appropriate reparation, and (4) creating a path to legal pardon (the perpetrators would need to ask for pardon, assume a new set of obligations, and not seek elected office). That approach contrasts with what the Salvadoran government did after the peace accords—namely, grant a general forgive-and-forget amnesty.

NICARAGUA

During a trip to Nicaragua in 2003, one of my guides was Adolfo Calero, a 1953 Notre Dame graduate who was prominent during that country's civil war as a leader of the Contras, the movement that arose in opposition to the Sandinista faction. He was the overall commander of the

Honduras-based guerrilla operation in the war, and he would make regular trips to the United States and elsewhere to lobby for financial and military support for the guerrillas. At lunch one day, he spoke of his familiarity with many members of the U.S. Congress and the Reagan administration who assisted the Contra cause, including Ollie North, who received the most publicity for his involvement in that affair, and John Poindexter, another Contra supporter.

That visit was my second to Nicaragua. On my first trip three years earlier, I was blown away by some of the incongruities I encountered. Here was a country that had experienced a long and violent civil war in which tens of thousands lost their lives, yet street life was generally safe and wealthy Nicaraguans did not have bodyguards. The main leaders of the two sides in the war—David Ortega for the Sandinistas, and Adolfo Calero for the Contras—were both serving in the congress and treating each other with politeness and courtesy. And by then the two sides that had financed the war—the United States and Russia—had largely lost interest in Nicaragua in the aftermath of the Cold War.

I paid a visit to the chancery office to meet with Cardinal Miguel Obando y Bravo, Archbishop of Managua. Although he comes from humble roots, he was much vilified when he opposed the Sandinistas and sided with Contras during the war. When he was made a cardinal in 1985, his selection was read as Vatican approval of his anti-Sandinista stand. I am sure that he is quite conservative theologically. Much of our conversation focused on his efforts to combat the aggressive proselytizing of various American-supported religious groups, such as the Mormons, Jehovah's Witnesses, and evangelicals. While competition for the loyalty of the poor people is probably a good wake-up call for the Catholic Church, there is a manifest anti-Catholicism in these groups, and seemingly unlimited funds from outside.

Nicaragua's old order was full of maldistribution of resources and a hard life for the poor. In the new Nicaragua, democracy has been restored, and ideologically driven killing has been controlled. But the future remains uncertain, and Nicaragua is still a poor country with huge human needs.

GUATEMALA

The extent of violence in Guatemala in the last few decades far exceeded that in the civil wars of either Nicaragua or El Salvador. Much of the violence was directed against Guatemala's Indian population, which constitutes a large portion of the country. Guatemala City still has a reputation as one of the more dangerous places in Latin America, particularly when it comes to kidnappings for money. During a visit in 2003, I expressed the hope that if I got kidnapped I wouldn't have to put my ransom payment up to a vote of the faculty.

During that visit my party was picked up by a Notre Dame alumnus who assured us that his SUV was bulletproof. He told us he himself had been kidnapped a few months before and held captive for ten days until his family paid a ransom. He said the ordeal was harder on his family than on him; he was not abused, although he was not given enough to eat.

When I visited in 1999, I was told that a fair amount of violence was still occurring in the country but that it was much more a matter of criminal behavior than ideologically driven. One of my hosts described having been held up on a country road by three masked men with AK-47 machine guns. Thankfully, they took money and no one was hurt.

The archdiocesan Office of Human Rights in Guatemala was ten years old at the time of that visit. It had begun as a legal assistance office and documentation center, but by 1999 the office was focused on the exhumation and forensic examination of corpses, providing mental health services for victims, and furnishing social services to the indigenous population. Digging up corpses from mass graves and conducting forensic evaluation of the circumstances and methods of their deaths is a complicated and heart-rending process, but in the Mayan tradition the ongoing relationship between the living and the dead is extremely important, and Mayans needed to know what happened to their relatives. Some had waited twenty years for news.

I saw a slide show with vivid pictures of corpses—some shot in the head, some killed with machete blows to the head, and some with their hands bound behind their backs. At the time of my visit, 360 corpses, including men and women, children and old people, had been exhumed.

The tombs were in isolated places, as if it were expected that they'd never be found.

In 1998, Juan Gerardi, the auxiliary bishop of Guatemala City, was murdered after he chaired the committee that issued a report *(Guatemala: Never Again)* on the human rights abuses during the conflict, with full documentation. I was given a copy in English to deliver to Notre Dame's Center for Civil and Human Rights. The government claimed that a priest had killed the bishop, but no one believed that.

HONDURAS

During a visit to Honduras in 2003, I was driven over one of the mountains ringing Tegucigalpa to a very impressive project that cares for babies, children, and young people who are dying of AIDS. The project, Casa Zulema, was started by Father Ramon Martinez, a Spanish diocesan priest from Grenada who, while working in a parish in Honduras, felt a call to begin this new ministry. The facility is right off a public park in the midst of the mountains, and it reminded me of a summer camp in Colorado. The buildings and furnishings were all donated by Spaniards.

Since the project began five years ago, they have buried more than one hundred babies and children. Assisting Father Ramon was a Honduran woman who had raised her own family and had training as an anesthesiology technician. At the time of my visit, the resident population was thirteen, with two in the hospital. The nurse described the emotional pain of tending to so many babies and children in the dying process.

Humberto Consenza, a Ph.D. from Notre Dame who serves as an adviser to the health ministry of the Honduran government, told me that almost all the country's AIDS cases were heterosexually transmitted, some from American military who were stationed in Honduras while the civil wars in El Salvador and Nicaragua were going on. Honduras, he added, had recently won a large grant from international agencies to combat AIDS, malaria, and other diseases.

Unlike its neighbors—Nicaragua, El Salvador, and Guatemala—Honduras has had no formal conflict in the last few decades. However, it was an arms supply area for guerrillas involved in those other conflicts, and there is still a heavy presence of weaponry. In Tegucigalpa I saw many watchmen with shotguns sitting outside houses, retail establishments, and public buildings. One of my hosts, Miguel Facussé, a Notre Dame grad from 1944 and a successful businessman, had a driver armed with a pistol, and a guard toting a machine gun, who accompanied him everywhere. A number of years ago, in a kidnap attempt his guard killed the kidnappers.

During one of my visits to Honduras, I took a seventy-minute helicopter flight from Tegucigalpa to the Mayan ruins at Copán at the eastern border of Honduras, next to Guatemala; if I had made the trip by car, it would have taken eight and a half hours. The ruins of Copán represent the highest artistic and cultural achievement of the ancient Maya civilization. Our guide was Ricardo Agurcia

Fasquelle, executive director of the Copán Association and a Honduran with an American doctorate in archeology who has spent most of his adult life overseeing the major dig on this site. Given his credentials, it was like touring the Promised Land with Moses.

COSTA RICA

For an area so close to the United States, Costa Rica is relatively unknown to most Americans. Yet streams of Central Americans, Costa Ricans among them, have sought refuge in the United States over the years, many undocumented. The movie *El Norte* captures their plight quite effectively.

One of my visits to Costa Rica was a trip sponsored by the Association of Catholic Colleges and Universities. Our group was centered at the United Nations University for Peace in San José, an institution created by the United Nations in 1980 that enjoys status comparable to an embassy. Its focus is primarily on graduate education and workshops, and it seeks to be a laboratory for courses and ideas. It views peace as more than disarmament, preferring to reflect on international social justice, environmental concerns, and other such topics.

In some ways, Costa Rica constitutes a living laboratory of experiments in peace. In a national poll, for example, 84 percent of Costa Ricans voted against establishing a military, and while the country has crime and other social ills like any society, Costa Ricans believe in conflict management. Just the fact that Costa Rica has seven living ex-presidents symbolizes the country's respect for life—no president or ex-president has ever been attacked or killed.

Some years after my first visit to the United Nations University for Peace, I stopped there again on another trip, and I had the same sense that I did originally: It is a place for idealists and dreamers. It plays a role, but it will never be a major actor.

PANAMA

I have traveled to Panama nearly a dozen times. That country furnishes the largest number of Notre Dame's undergraduate-program alumni of any country outside the United States. This was very much the result of the influence of the late Archbishop Mark McGrath, C.S.C., who was head of the Church in Panama City for many years and a major figure at the Second Vatican Council. He fostered Panamanian students coming to Notre Dame and contributed to our good relationship with the Catholic University of Panama. Since his death, we have been trying to build up scholarship funds in his honor.

Archbishop McGrath is buried in a flat tomb next to his predecessors in the cathedral in Panama City, an old church in need of renovation but still an active place of worship. A painting of the archbishop sits on a tripod on top of the tomb, with an inscription in Spanish summarizing of his life and ministry. While praying at his tomb during one of my trips, I recalled vividly earlier times I spent with him in Panama. One such time was in January 1995, when he hosted me for a small, enjoyable dinner with some friends in his retirement home on the grounds of a group of religious sisters. The house contained an office, a bedroom, a small chapel, a dining room, and an open-air terrace; on the wall were pictures of the bishops at Vatican II, the meeting of the Latin American bishops at Puebla, and other mementos in his life. Mark was a wonderful host that evening. Overall, he was truly a great churchman who died from Parkinson's disease with dignity and grace.

I feel quite at home with the Panamanian friends we have made through the years. A couple of them are on the University's Latin American and Caribbean Advisory Council. As a group, they have a deep love for Notre Dame and are well informed about events on campus.

During a visit I made to Panama in 1995, the image of Manuel Noriega, the former dictator, still loomed large. There is no doubt that Noriega was a cutthroat military leader and was involved in drug-dealing and widespread corruption. During his regime, Panama fell into wide social inequity and class barriers, and it seems likely that the CIA was involved with Noriega and protected him. An American invasion of Panama in 1989–90 led to Noriega's capture and extradition to Florida, where he was convicted of drug charges and given a forty-year sentence. American assistance propped up the interim government and led to the cleanest elections in Panamanian history.

Through the American Embassy during that winter 1995 trip, I arranged for a tour of the camps where some 8,600 Cuban exiles were being housed in four tent cities. Except for a handful, all had originally been housed at Guantánamo Bay. When the numbers at Guantánamo grew too large, the only country willing to provide temporary refuge was Panama, with the provision that the site be American-controlled. At the time of my visit, the Panamanian government had recently set a deadline for all the Cubans to be out, and this had created a sense of panic and desperation in the camps. The most likely alternatives for those who did not qualify for entry into the United States—the majority of prisoners—were being returned to Guantánamo, choosing to go back to Cuba, or seeking a third country. I did not know if I would be seeing a minor replay of *Schindler's List* during my visit, but it turned out that the American military authorities and an embassy aide could not have been more forthcoming.

A month before my visit, there had been riots at the camps, and many American servicemen were injured by thrown rocks and hand-to-hand battles with sticks and other implements. Since then, the military presence had been significantly increased, and armed guards patrolled both inside and outside the camps. Eighty-four percent of the camp inmates were men, 11 were women, and 5 percent were children. It was costing eight dollars a day to feed each person, better than they had eaten in Cuba, I was told.

I visited the camp's medical facilities, which were first-rate for a field unit and provided dental care and simple surgery. The need I found most surprising was for a rather large mental illness unit—the level of stress and depression in the camps was quite high. An Irish-Catholic Army captain from Boston walked me through one camp, with the Cubans walking about freely. Some were playing soccer or basketball, and many were watching a large television in an open tent. They were not overtly hostile but they were reserved. Before leaving the camp, we met with a delegation of Cuban male leaders. The gist of their message was that they were desperate—they had risked their lives seeking freedom in the United States, but because someone changed the rules they were now prisoners facing the threat of forced return to Guantánamo. They said they would rather die than go back. It was impossible to hear their story and not be moved. They gave us some handwritten letters from the camp residents, pleading for help.

It is difficult to know what to say about such a heartwrenching dilemma. The problem of refugees and displaced persons remains a worldwide quandary, and political sentiment in the United States, even before the World Trade Center attacks, was turning against relatively open borders.

CUBA

A few months before I visited Cuba in the spring of 2002, I watched *Thirteen Days*, the cinematic portrayal of the Cuban missile episode. I thought it captured well the sense of crisis that shook the United States in 1962, when President John F. Kennedy announced on national television that

Soviet nuclear missiles on Cuban soil were targeted at the United States. I remember the air-raid drills at school and the sense that we were all threatened, so it seemed almost eerie that I was in Cuba, still under Castro, these many years later. The trip was arranged for our School of Architecture's advisory council and was led by a Cuban-American architecture faculty member, Victor Deupi. Despite the official U.S. boycott of the island, the government is willing to approve several types of trips to Cuba, including trips for educational purposes.

We stayed at the Nacional Hotel in Havana, kind of like the huge, old classic hotels in Miami Beach. It was on a hill with a gentle slope down to the waterfront, and directly beneath my eighth-floor room was a highway that hugged the shoreline. Our cab driver from the airport spoke English but said American accents are sometimes hard for him since he learned British pronunciation in school. At dinner in a local restaurant, about half the diners were Cuban, and there were a good number of Americans as well.

Pope John Paul II's visit in 1998 was a major event for Cuba. Since then, the Church has had a little more room to function. The big pastoral problem now is forty years of Leninism. Although young people don't believe in Communism, we were told, they seem to lack deep-seated values of any kind. The Castro government promotes the notion that Santería is a native Cuban form of worship, because it keeps the Catholic Church from having a base in poor neighborhoods. The pastoral strategy has been to adopt as much of the native Santería religious traditions and practices as possible and then try to purify them.

Ironically, some churchless Europeans come to Cuba to participate in Santería initiation rites; it is a kind of New-Age-meets-the-occult attraction. Catholic laypeople now have more freedom to serve in professions like education and medicine, but you still have to be a Communist Party member to get a top administrative job.

We toured Old Havana, viewing well-restored areas and poor neighborhoods in the old slave quarters. The Church of Saint Francis is now a concert hall and museum; where the main altar was is a grand piano with a religious painting behind it and a large, gaunt crucifix hanging down from above—an odd juxtaposition of the secular and the religious. The Convent of Saint Clare, a square block in size, is now a center for the restoration of ancient structures; in its prime, it was home to one hundred nuns and servants. There was a proliferation of cafes and outdoor restaurants, some with live entertainment. We spotted large numbers of European tourists, and some Americans and Latin Americans. Credit cards were not accepted, so Americans had to carry dollars to pay for meals and other things. Sometimes our group looked like bookies with our wads of bills. We felt safe walking around, and we sensed no hostility to Americans.

The capitol, one of whose co-designers was a graduate of Notre Dame's School of Architecture, was built in 1925 in a style resembling the U.S. Capitol, with a high dome and two adjacent wings. It is a beautiful structure, though somewhat overstated for the size and power of the country. The building does not have any government function under the present regime.

We saw only one representation of the hammer-and-sickle symbol of the old U.S.S.R. during our visit, but there was no limit to the number of revolutionary slogans painted on walls. Cuban military were around, but it was really the police who seemed to assume control of every-day life. At intersections, the police stopped drivers and pedestrians to ask for identification—a phenomenon that prevails in totalitarian and/or corrupt societies. Tourists usually do not have to deal with it.

Castro's control over Cuban society is apparently all-encompassing. Block patrols spy on their neighbors. Police are everywhere, and Cubans are asked frequently to show identification, especially the young men. Cuban staff workers at the American Embassy (where the phones are tapped and the mail is read) have to be approved by the Cuban government. For many Cubans, Castro is the known enemy, and they fear that the future could be worse. One island story goes that Castro was presented with a gift of a four-hundred-year old turtle from the Galápagos Islands. He said, "That's the problem with pets. Just when you get close to them, they die." In other words, how long can Castro last?

Possible future scenarios: (1) Castro is replaced by someone like himself, only younger; (2) Raoul Castro, his younger brother, takes over; (3) Cuban-Americans play a significant role in a transition; (4) there is a prompt and peaceful transition to democracy. The official succession plan is that Raoul Castro will take over for Fidel, but he lacks charisma, and there is suspicion that he also lacks popular support.

Meanwhile, the average Cuban is more concerned about economic realities than civil liberties. In the black market you can get anything you want if you have the money or know where to find it. People steal on their jobs. Access to things to resell is coveted, and this creates a condition where everyone is engaged in behavior for which they could be arrested, which reinforces the power of the regime.

Whether we like it or not, Fidel is a survivor and continues to influence the United States. I hope and pray that Cuba can make a peaceful transition to a democratic government committed to the well-being of all its people. In the meantime, my sense is that the more the island opens up to the outside world, the better the chances that the common good will be served.

SOUTH AMERICA

BRAZIL

Rio de Janeiro is one of the most beautiful cities in the world, rivaling Sydney, Hong Kong, and San Francisco for beaches, high mountain overlooks, public parks, and distinctive lifestyle. It is well known, of course, for its Carnival, its feasts, and a fun-loving lifestyle, as well as skimpy bathing suits and a religious mix of Catholicism and traditional African religions. But in addition to great wealth, culture, and luxury, Rio has a dark underside. Jutting up into the hills are *favelas*, or slums, which house many of the city's poor. In these areas, violence is common and life is cheap.

I visited a performing arts project in one of the more notorious *favelas*, and although it was only a five-minute drive from my hotel, it took me to a starkly different reality. We drove up, up, and up through a tough neighborhood where young people were playing or walking while the middle and older generations were sitting around in small groups. The social structure in these slums has been compared to a mafia village in Sicily. We did not need to fear being held up or having bags taken from our van, because the local drug gang knew who we were. When our group took a walk through the neighborhood with two of the older kids, we were objects of curiosity but everyone was friendly.

At a five-story building that serves as a social center and creative arts school for local kids, we were entertained by a ballet group of ten teenage girls dressed in white leotards, black skirts, and white ballet shoes. Most of the children were racially black, with some differences of shade. After the dance, we watched an elaborate play full of social commentary on such matters as drug and alcohol use, police violence, and the sustained grief of survivors. The overall message was that society needs to do better by its children. From the upper floor of the building, we could see most of the *favela* and, in the distance, some of the great beaches of the world.

CHILE

During a trip to Chile in 1985 while the dictator Augusto Pinochet Ugarte was still in power, I was told of a non-violent protest group focusing on the issue of torture in which a lot of priests and nuns were involved. Their strategy was to demonstrate in some crowded public place in Santiago without notifying the authorities and then disappear after five to ten minutes. The religious motivation of the majority of participants probably prevented more violent confrontations. The police (derogatorily called *pacos*) were basically hostile in those days. They were assigned to areas of the country not native to them, and given training that they interpreted as a mandate to control dissent by whatever methods worked. In the mid-1980s they would hover over the *poblaciones* late at night in helicopters and shine searchlights down while army troops and police on the ground sealed off the exits. Then they would make wholesale arrests, shoot up a neighborhood, and disappear into the night.

Torture under Pinochet was going on in wholesale fashion, employing methods so effective that few could resist. Some of it was done by the police, some by the military, and some by clandestine right-wing groups—which is not to say that the left in other parts of the world is incapable of the same tactics; the Stalinist legacy at that time still lived on in Russia. The obvious question for Americans was what the U.S. government thought of such human rights abuses. Was anything acceptable in the name of anti-Communism?

In spite of the oppressive atmosphere, Pinochet jokes circulated, for example: President Reagan, Pope John Paul II, a hippie, and General Pinochet are passengers on a plane when the pilot announces it is going to crash. The problem is, there are only three parachute packs. President Reagan declares that he is the head of the most powerful nation on earth and therefore should jump first. He picks up a pack and jumps. Next General Pinochet announces that he is the most intelligent president in the world, and he picks up a pack and jumps. The Pope offers to let the hippie take the final pack, since it is proper for the Pope to give his life for others. But the hippie tells the Pope not to worry—the most intelligent president in the world had grabbed the hippie's backpack instead of a parachute. As many Chileans told me, you need a sense of humor to survive under a dictatorship.

Holy Cross has had priests in Chile for many years, and eleven of its members were expelled during the Pinochet years. A Holy Cross Associates program has also operated in Chile for years. These domestic volunteers, mostly recently graduated Notre Dame students, commit themselves to a year of service, living together in a simple lifestyle in groups of three, four, or five. They cook for themselves, pray together, and have weekly meetings with a coordinator from the local Holy Cross community. They receive a small salary from the community, though most of their funds come from their work situations. Most groups are about half male and half female. Their work assignments are negotiated individually, depending on their backgrounds and interests. Examples would be alcohol counseling, teaching grade school, organizational development with volunteer service groups, and parish pastoral work. Most are involved with the poor, the young, the addicted, or some other needful segment of the population. They are properly prepared in the language when they arrive.

The national climate was much more relaxed for my second visit to Chile in 1990, after a successful plebiscite against General Pinochet and the election of Patricio Aylwin as president. Hope was in the air with the promise of an end to the bloody and oppressive military rule. Five years later, Chile's major dilemma was what to do about the military leaders who were under indictment for human rights abuses in the Pinochet years. President Aylwin by then had literally brought the country back from the brink of perpetual hatred and endemic violence. Supported by a broad coalition of parties, he stressed unity and forgiveness, truth and responsibility—but truth above all, insofar as holding the military responsible was concerned.

There are many issues that span the Americas— language, race, pervasive poverty, out-migration, and religion. In Latin American history, the Catholic Church was the church of the establishment and had a direct relationship to the state, a fact that alienates most of the left. There is also a growing Pentecostal movement that pictures the Catholic Church as "The Beast" from the Book of Revelation; these people are not open to dialogue. Opus Dei and the Legionnaires of Christ, both conservative Catholic movements, are strong in Chile. The creation of a new Jesuit university was perceived as a sign that the Catholic University of Chile had been taken over by Opus Dei.

This conservative backlash may be a reaction to the progressive orientation of the Church under Pinochet. During the dictatorship, the two main institutions in the country were the army and the Church, and the main vehicle for investigating abuses of civil and human rights was the Catholic Vicariate of Solidarity. Many clerics feel that the Church must engage in missionary outreach and be in dialogue with the culture. They say the Church's message has been too moralistic and needs more emphasis on solidarity, compassion, and a spirit of cooperation.

Chile has been a social laboratory over the last fifty years. It has gone from democracy to an elected Marxist president to a military dictatorship to a democratic government. The big problem for the Church is how to function in a more pluralistic society. The problem of the poor is especially urgent.

AFRICA

CAMEROON

A meeting of the International Federation of Catholic Universities (IFCU) took me to Cameroon, Africa, in 1996. That country was chosen as our meeting place for two reasons: Most of us on the federation council had never been to black Africa and we wanted a firsthand experience; also, we wanted to offer moral support to the fledgling Catholic University in Yaoundé, the capital of Cameroon.

Before leaving home, I took shots for yellow fever, meningitis, tetanus, and a few odds and ends. In addition, I began a regimen of once-a-week malaria pills. The fact that there had been outbreaks of the Ebola virus a country or two away from Cameroon grabs your attention. I promised that I would not eat monkey brains if I could avoid it.

The first thing to say about traveling to West Africa is that it is not easy. My original flight plan was Chicago to Brussels to Douala, Cameroon's largest city and main port. From there I was to fly to Yaoundé in the interior, with no layover. But then it turned out that I needed to stay overnight in Douala.

The temperature in Douala when I arrived was in the nineties, and it was humid. Although the airport is rather large, the only large plane I saw was the one I flew in on. The baggage area was full of porters, hotel representatives, and tour guides, and a small band played calypso-style music off in a corner. I was delighted to see a man with a sign for my hotel, which turned out to be quite comfortable. During the night, I received a phone call telling me that my 8:00 A.M. flight to Yaoundé had been canceled and that I'd been rebooked on a noon flight. They never said it would be easy to get to Yaoundé.

At the airport around noon, the Air Cameroon staff was checking in a flight to Nairobi, but beyond that nothing was happening. Eventually I was informed that there were mechanical problems on my flight; now the earliest we might take off was 6:00 P.M., and even that was not certain. Some baggage handlers recommended either taking a bus to Yaoundé or riding with one of their friends for the equivalent of one hundred dollars. I decided on the bus.

The three-and-a-half-hour bus trip was a real gift, because I got to see the main route between the two largest cities in the country. Scenes along the way included semis hauling gigantic logs, a number of trucks broken down on the side of the road (God knows how they get fixed), and large numbers of schoolchildren as little as kindergartners walking right next to the highway on their way home from school. We stopped at about ten tollbooth-style passage points, and the ones near Yaoundé were staffed by soldiers with rifles. We passed countless people walking from one place to another—women with packages on their heads and men carrying bolo knives. Some women and a few men were traditionally garbed with bright colors and sweeping design, but the majority had Western-style outfits.

Yaoundé was clearly where the money was. There were a few twenty-story buildings, a number of modern hotels, and a crowded street scene. Right below my hotel was a golf course with sand greens. I could see puffs of smoke around the area, a sign of slash-and-burn agriculture.

Being in Africa naturally raises questions about the future of that continent. In many places the social, economic, and political reality is rather depressing, with violence and social dislocation all too common. AIDS remains rampant, outbreaks of disease are frequent, and there are places where Islam and Christianity are facing off in a hostile fashion. Potentially, the richest country in black Africa, outside of South Africa, should be Nigeria, but it has been a center of corruption, tribal rivalries, and bad government.

In Cameroon there are 150 separate tribal languages but only three major ones in the Yaoundé area. The country is more than 50 percent Christian and probably has a more positive relationship with the Muslim community than anywhere else in Africa. When the Pope visited Yaoundé, a Muslim representative agreed to say a few words.

The Holy Cross community has been in Africa since the 1950s (leaving aside a presence in Algeria in our early history). We started in Uganda, Kenya, and Ghana, and more recently we've been in Rwanda, where four of our brother candidates and one priest were killed—the candidates because they were of the wrong tribal group, and the French Canadian priest for unknown reasons. At the beginning of our time in Africa, we did not accept African vocations, partly in order to maintain good relations with the diocesan clergy and partly out of fear of vocations motivated by upward mobility. Now we have a growing number of candidates and professed members.

In a phone conversation with the American cultural attaché in Yaoundé regarding my return flights, the attaché said that Air Cameroon was notoriously unreliable—almost a mythical airline that constantly delays and cancels flights; they had a crash several months ago and lost one-quarter of their fleet (one plane out of four). He recommended driving to Douala, though not at night. I am usually a fearless traveler, but I did not feel good about my options.

I decided to take the bus back to Douala. Checking out of the hotel, I asked the desk clerk to call a cab to take me to the bus station. The first problem, he said, was that there were many bus companies. I told him to pick a good one. The cab deposited me at a chaotic-looking station with parking room for one bus. A young man in a kind of Boy Scout uniform grabbed my bags and pointed me inside. That was the first risk: Would my bags be there when I came back outside?

There were about twenty people in the ticket line. Because I don't speak French, I simply handed over the amount of money I knew the trip cost and hoped for the best. Boarding the bus, I carried one small bag with me and thought I saw the attendant put the other one in the hold, though I wasn't sure. The bus's air conditioner did not work, and a loudspeaker constantly played music— Cameroon rap and American and French singers.

At Douala my other bag turned out to be in the hold, and when I arrived at the airport around 8:30 for my 11:15 A.M. flight I was gratified to find other early passengers in evidence—a good sign that my journey was not in vain.

As it turned out, we left just about on time with a full flight. Why was I worried?

My visit was worth the travel glitches. I experienced no great shock with regard to being in a predominantly black society, since in that regard urban life in the States often has this same characteristic. In the campus chapel at the Catholic University in Yaoundé, the altar, lectern, benches, tabernacle, and the stained glass above the altar all had African motifs or faces. There was a large mural behind the altar with Jesus, Peter, and John depicted at the Last Supper with local faces and garb.

Although I saw only one African country, Cameroon's positive and negative features are probably typical of this part of the world. What the continent seems to need most of all is hope. Both education and the Church must play a role in this regard, but in the end it will require African leadership; international agencies can assist but not impose. God willing, Africa can take a positive turn, as many parts of Asia and Latin America have.

DOWN UNDER

AUSTRALIA

To start a university in the late twentieth century, particularly a private one, might seem like the project of fools. Nevertheless, there was something exciting and challenging about the venture called Notre Dame Australia. Our involvement in that institution on Australia's west coast began in 1987 when Ted Hesburgh and Ned Joyce stopped in Perth during a world cruise after their retirement. Ted's brother Jim had done some business with an Aussie businessman named Denis Horgan, who, along with Peter Tannock, an Australian educator, had a dream of establishing a Catholic university in Western Australia, and Ted and Ned encouraged the two men to come and visit us in South Bend. After looking at many other Catholic institutions in Europe and the States, they decided they wanted to use us as a model and solicited our assistance.

The result was that several Notre Dame officers and I visited Perth/Fremantle in the summer of 1988 after attending an IFCU Assembly in Jakarta, Indonesia. All of us were immediately struck by the possibilities and excited by the opportunity to assist in the project. I made several subsequent trips to Australia and in 1991 was present for the inauguration of the new university. Although Notre Dame Indiana, as they call us in Australia, has no formal or financial responsibility for Notre Dame Australia, we function as advisers and we send undergraduate students there to study. As an additional form of assistance, Dave Link, former dean of our law school, served as NDA's first vice-chancellor/president.

My first visit in 1988 was my introduction to the globe's smallest continent. Perth is the regional capital of Western Australia, which covers an area three times the size of Texas. Australia is an interesting place for ecological study. Other than the dingo dog, most of the continent's other animals—cows, horses, sheep, cats, rabbits, and so on—were introduced after western settlers arrived. There are ten types of deadly snakes. Of course, kangaroos are identified with the country, as are koala bears.

The Outback is a formidable place, resembling a mix of West Texas, Utah, and Arizona. The primary vegetation is clumps of bushes and small trees in the midst of tracts of brown or reddish clay. In some sections there are pools or lakes of water, depending on the season. The overall impression is that the faint of heart should avoid living there. Space is endless and people are few and widely separated.

The aborigines are a tragic story. A nomadic people who for much of their history lived in the bush, they are now attracted to small towns, where they survive on the welfare system and spend much of the day just sitting around. Alcoholism is rampant, and there is a high incidence of family violence, barroom fights, traffic accidents, and the like. The number of aborigines who have been successfully integrated into the trained work force is very small. The Catholic Church is deeply involved in outreach programs, and the state provides basics like schools, hospitals, and the rudiments of local government, but no one seems very confident that much progress has been made.

Citizens of Western Australia are conscious of how far away they are from the rest of civilization, and that leads to a spirit of self-sufficiency and enterprise but also to a degree of isolation. Visitors in the west are well treated, at least in part because they provide contact with the outside world.

Australia is the most sports-oriented society I have encountered. The major sports on television are Aussie football, rugby, soccer, and cricket, but tennis, swimming, and golf are popular participant and spectator sports. Basketball is probably the fastest-growing sport.

Australian-style English presents no real problems for Americans. The spelling conforms to the British system ("labor" becomes "labour"), and some of the terms vary ("lift" for "elevator"). The pronunciation is British ("shedule" for "schedule"). But the hardest part is those distinctively Australian idioms that make no sense until you have the background. For instance, the song "Waltzing Matilda" is not about dancing with a woman but about carrying a backpack around on a trek through the Outback.

The Caucasian presence in Australia is very much connected to the effort in the British Empire to establish prison colonies, as it did, for example, in Georgia and Maryland. These prisoners were not quite slaves, because their terms eventually ended and there were some limits on their work conditions. Between 1788 and 1868, some 168,000 convicts were sent to Australia, of whom 25,000 were Irish. Western Australia was the last area to stop the system. The first priests came in 1821 to pastor the Irish. At the end of World War II, 98 percent of Australia's white population had roots in the British Isles and Ireland.

Anthropologists estimate that the Aboriginal (the word means "from the beginning") people came to Australia 50,000 to 70,000 years ago, when the shape of the continent was different and the seas between South Asia and Australia were shallower, allowing easier water passage; Tasmania was connected to the mainland then. The settlers survived an Ice Age, and when the snow melted, the seas rose and they were cut off. Eventually, they spread over the continent and developed a unique lifestyle. When the Europeans arrived, there were about 750,000 nomadic aboriginals with 750 different language groups and a hunter-gatherer existence.

Aboriginal culture was rigid and very vulnerable to white culture. The people were vulnerable to disease, and sugar was a dietary risk. The arrival of television changed their lives dramatically: They abandoned hunting and gathering, and their children often do not speak the tribal languages.

During one of my Australian visits, I traveled to two Aboriginal communities. If you look at a map of Australia, find Broome and then draw a line straight east for two to two and a half hours of flying time—that's where we went. Maybe Antarctica and Siberia are more isolated, but between Broome and Mulan/Balgo there are no towns, no airports, one road, and almost no people. Our pilot was a woman in her twenties named Tammie. Raised in the Outback, Tammie had flown since she was fourteen and was an accomplished bush pilot. Our twin-prop Cessna 310 carried extra fuel tanks because there was no place to refuel on our route.

We landed on a good airstrip next to the aboriginal community in Mulan, where 150 people live in ramshackle buildings. But the common areas like the school and the medical clinic and the offices were well maintained and serviceable, and there was even a Chinese take-out place. Some of the elders we met complained that young people don't follow the old ways or respect their elders. Many of the elders cannot read or write, although now there are courses for them and they seemed pleased about that. Most of the adults were in bare feet; the men wore shorts or long pants, the women wore dresses or blouses with skirts. Many of the adults were overweight. The elders said they'd like to have an art center, and a new outdoor basketball court is being built. The settlement made a decision four years earlier to make it a "no grog"—that is, "no alcohol"—community. There was a chapel area, and a Jesuit priest from Balgo came for Mass.

Balgo, a twenty-minute flight from Mulan, is a "large" community of 350. One of the programs in Balgo trains men to be able to fix their own houses and teaches adult women sewing and secretarial skills. Our Aborigine guide (who wore a Pittsburgh Steelers hat) took us to an isolated site containing ancient cave drawings. To get there we had to make our way through prickly grass, down a ravine, along a dry riverbed, and up to the area where the drawings were found. The snake image was the most common. The site was an ancient watering hole with a small pool of water. With a little imagination, you could sense the sacredness of the place. On the way back to the Land Rover, I slipped and sustained a few minor abrasions on my arm and leg. I wanted to concoct a heroic tale about how I fended off a herd of wild kangaroo, but I figured no one would buy it.

I returned from the visit with some lasting impressions: beautiful, smiling children in the classrooms; four girls having their hair done by one of the women; mousy-looking dogs lying around; men sitting in groups and watching the world go by; the Jesuit priest showing us the beautiful art in the European-style church, which was hardly ever used because people like to worship outside; trash and other junk strewn about as if it made no difference; a young Aborigine singing a song he had composed about some white boys who died in the desert; the obvious dedication of the religious men and women who staff the communities, try out new programs, seek additional resources, and fight the good fight; the sense of lethargy and dispiritedness that is difficult to overcome when a nomadic culture settles in one spot and lives on federal monies; the creativity and spark that comes through Aboriginal art.

On another visit to Australia, I visited Kalumburu in the far reaches of Western Australia. It's a community of four hundred Aboriginals that is closer to Timor and Indonesia than to Perth or Brisbane. When the Benedictines came to the area in 1918, the Aboriginals were at first hostile, and at one point they attacked the priests and ran the abbot through with a spear. Because Europeans were white-skinned, the natives believed they were either cave people or dead people. The missionaries were puzzled by the relative absence of children until they found out that the Aborigines did not understand the connection between sexual expression and pregnancy. In addition, some ascetic cults encouraged sexual mutilation. The area is now under government control, with the religious community playing only a pastoral and educational role.

We paid a visit to a rock gorge in the King Edward River a few miles from the mission to see an 18,000-year-old set of rock paintings on ledges. The figures were long and thin, almost playful, and some had boomerangs in their hands. The site may have been used for initiation rites—it is readily accessible, close to water, and the rock overhangs would have provided protection against the rain.

Bungle Bungles is a national park in Western Australia that contains an extraordinary geological mountain range of sandstone shaped over millions of years into striped formations, alternately red and black. Some of the formations resemble gigantic honeycombs, and throughout the park there are deep gorges. We took a thirty-minute helicopter flight over the park, and it was like viewing a succession of smaller Grand Canyons whose stones gave off a tawny red in the morning sun. When we landed, we piled into in a van that took about an hour to reach the walking area, and then we walked for forty-five minutes into Cathedral Gorge. At the end of the gorge is a dead-end amphitheater effect where some massive stone plates have fallen. We sang one verse of the Notre Dame Victory March to hear the echo. There are several streams and one wide river in the park, but there is almost no water left. The sandstone erodes regularly in heavy rains.

Australian stereotypes say this about the continent: Perth is the cowboys; Melbourne is the old money; Sydney is the entrepreneurial center; Queensland, the tropical state in the northeast, is the crooks. Australians appear to dislike Japanese tourists, perhaps because they remind them of perceived or real threats to the north.

NEW ZEALAND

A journey I took from Madrid, Spain, to Christchurch, New Zealand, in 1999 would have taken months at earlier times in human history. Even in the jet age it was a trek to do it nonstop, but it helped to have a little luck along the way. For example, I knew I had to check my big bag in Madrid, but my connection time in Paris was only a little over an hour and previous experience with baggage transfers at De Gaulle Airport gave me reason to worry— all I needed was to have one of my bags end up on a different continent. The clerk at the Air France desk in Madrid suggested I go standby for an earlier flight, and when the time came I jumped ahead of a bunch of other standby passengers. Before they closed the plane door there was a dispute about too many passengers onboard and I fully expected them to kick me off, but no one looked my way. (At that point I was like one of my students in class who doesn't want to be called on—I never glanced up.) The flight to Paris made it with only a small delay and gave me a three-hour window for the bag to be transferred.

The flight from Paris to Tokyo took twelve hours and thirty minutes and arrived right on time. I lucked out again, because the seat next to me in business class was empty. Not only could I put my reading material there, but it also was easier to sleep and no one wanted to crawl past me to go to the bathroom. On the flight from Tokyo to Christchurch, which took eleven hours and ten minutes, I ended up again with an empty seat next to me. My total travel time from Madrid to Christchurch was more than thirty hours. And when the checked baggage came out of the maw of the snaking line, wonder of wonders, there was my bag.

Bill Beauchamp met me at Christchurch, and we rented a car for the seven-hour drive to Te Anau, the jumping-off point for Milford Sound. It probably sounds crazy to drive so far, after my long flights, but along the way we were able to see about half of South Island, which by consensus has some of the best scenery on earth.

The first part of our trip took us straight down the east coast to Timaru, through mainly small towns on a two-lane highway. We crossed wide riverbeds with little water in them and saw signs along the road warning of a high risk of forest fire. As we drove westward from Timaru, the terrain went from arid and bleak to pockets of trees and vegetation near streams, rivers, and lakes. The farther west we went, the more vegetation we encountered. One town, Cromwell, seemed to be the orchard capital of New Zealand. We also saw thousands and thousands of sheep and deer, and some cattle, and along the way we passed groups of motorcyclists who looked like the characters in the *Mad Max* movie series, which was filmed in the Outback of Australia. The atmosphere was amazingly pollution-free.

In Te Anau it rained all night, drumming on the tin roof of our motel, and we decided to hang around the motel for a while in the morning to see if the rain would let up. A woman in the restaurant said it was the area's first rain in quite a while, but Milford Sound gets 30 feet of rain a year, so rainy days cannot be too unusual. There were some American tourists at our motel, and I watched small groups of backpackers with rain gear walking next to the highway; they call this getting in touch with nature.

The southwest coast of South Island is called Fiordland, and there is only one road to get from Te Anau to Milford Sound. The rain had a fortuitous effect for us, because it inundated the mountains and produced hundreds of cascading waterfalls on our drive to Milford Sound. I have never before seen so many waterfalls, and the route was green, lush, and progressively more spectacular.

Milford Sound is on a fiord at the base of high mountains and offers overnight accommodations for those inclined to stay. Five or six boats provide tours through the Sound, but we got there too late for a ride. We took a walk along a path that passed two waterfalls, one of which was so strong that you'd get soaked if you got too close. Mitre Peak (5,560 feet) is one of the highest mountains in the world, rising directly from the ocean floor. Mount Pembroke (6,500 feet) is permanently snowcapped and has a glacier. The whole park is one of the best nature preserves in the world, with the added attraction of being accessible and safe.

At gas stations, stores, and motels, New Zealanders (alias Kiwis) like to engage you in conversation. The country is famous for its sheep, which outnumber people many times over. All they seem to do is eat, and occasionally look up with indifference at passing cars. Little do they know what is in store for them, since on the road we passed many semis carrying sheep to market.

In Christchurch, a city known for its floral tradition, we took a stroll through the botanical gardens. Then we had dinner at a pub where the tradition seemed to be smashing used bottles into a large receptacle. It was a little jarring in the midst of dinner.

THE FAR EAST

CHINA

To travel to China is to penetrate a world that was off-limits to Westerners until President Nixon's initiative in 1972. The Forbidden City in the heart of Beijing is truly one of the human-made wonders of the world.

On my first visit in 1987, Beijing impressed me as a city of the future, like San Diego or Phoenix. At that time it was a city of four million bikes—one and a half bikes for every household. Some of the streets had separate bike lanes, and the sidewalks were full of bike racks. Fashion was in, and the days of the Mao jacket and unisex clothes had been left behind. High value was placed on family life; everywhere I went I observed the deep bonds across generations. In a one-child policy this may on occasion lead to overindulgence, but it is surely preferable to the problems of domestic violence, abandonment, and affective disinterest that plague so much of American society. The Chinese clearly love their children and sacrifice continually for their best interest.

The Chinese banquet, I discovered, is a highly refined art; it is best not to eat anything else the same day, lest one's stomach burst. Two banquets in one day make one understand how the Romans resorted to regurgitation. The Chinese love their parks and flowers, and nature is now being cultivated systematically in ways that were neglected during the Cultural Revolution. The Chinese army seemed to be primarily an employment agency; at any given moment, half the army appeared to be on holiday. Women were said to be officially liberated in China—equal pay for equal work—and in fact they were visible in most professions, yet there still seemed to be many subtle differences, especially in leadership roles and in rural settings.

China has clearly made a decision to invest heavily in an elite notion of higher education, based more on the British or French model than the American or Russian one. Many of their brightest students study abroad in America, Europe, and Japan; when they return, they give the quality of research a real boost, provided the government can subsidize the necessary facilities. In the field of education, China is trying to make up for all that was lost during the Cultural Revolution.

A Mass that I attended in the Catholic cathedral was an extraordinary experience. The priest wore traditional vestments and had his back to the people; there were two altar boys, bells for the Consecration, and Communion taken on the tongue kneeling at the Communion rail. I received Communion with the other Americans in my party, and we drew a few glances from the congregation. Many worshipers used missals during Mass, and a few had rosaries. Above the altar was a large mural of the Blessed Mother surrounded by artificial roses. A confessional in the back was in use during Mass.

I experienced a real sense of solidarity with this oft-persecuted church. The worshipers' piety was obviously genuine. A choir sang a series of Latin and Chinese hymns, and many in the congregation joined in. Benediction of the Blessed Sacrament followed Mass: a lot of incense and the regular ritual. At a statue of Mary in the cathedral courtyard after Mass, about a dozen people paused to pray.

When I paid a second visit to China in 1996, I was curious to see how much things had changed. One big difference was that Beijing had gone from a city where bicycles reigned to a city with four concentric circles of motor expressways, three or four lanes wide in each direction, and many more cars, taxis, and buses. There were still plenty of bikes and special lanes for them, but a new subway and the growth of motorized transportation were changing all that. In 1987, Beijing struck me as one gigantic building project. In 1996, many modern high-rise structures were in place and the architecture was quite attractive.

When I think back, my vague impression of China in pre-Nixon days was forged by images from the Korean War and news clips of people in massive rallies. All was mystery, and I had no sense of the Chinese as individual people engaged in everyday affairs. Demystification of China is relatively easy when one is in Beijing. I had nice accommodations and a driver and guides to take me around, and the people I met were uniformly friendly and courteous. There was no visible military presence, although I passed some military barracks where I saw soldiers drilling. This country that was off-limits to Westerners for so long was now neither as foreboding nor quite as mysterious as I once thought.

The Great Wall, certifiably one of the human-made wonders of the world, lives up to expectations. It must have been constructed against great odds and with a large loss of life. Now it stands as an early-day Maginot Line. One sign of modern China was the number of hawkers of trinkets and cards I encountered at way-stations along the Wall.

Hangzhou, southwest of Shanghai on the coast and once China's capital, is considered one of the most beautiful cities in China. The Lin Yin shrine there contains several large Buddhist pagodas and spacious gardens. When I was there, people were lighting candles in front of the Buddha and kneeling in prayer.

Some thoughts about the matter of religion in China: It goes without saying that from 1917 on, Marxist-Leninist regimes have been hostile to religion. The famous expression of Marx that "religion is the opiate of the people" conveys the view that religion is a structured way of keeping the poor oppressed and that the churches have been aligned historically with the ruling classes. In this view, it is only when Communism offers a radical vision of a better life in this world that the people can rise up and take control of their destiny. But the result of that ideology has been persecution, martyrdom, and marginalization.

After the Chinese Revolution in 1948, Christians, Buddhists, Muslims, and adherents of all faiths were suppressed, imprisoned, and/or killed. But after the fervor of the early purges, puppet churches with their own ecclesial structures and services were set up. In recent years a two-tiered structure has developed in the universe of Chinese Catholics. The government gives official approbation to the so-called Patriotic Catholic Church (although many of its members, including its leaders, have been persecuted and imprisoned), but there is also an underground church, which is allowed to function quietly and without government recognition. Informers report on the substance of homilies and other underground church activities, however, and jail is an ever-present threat for priests. The risk is also great for those who worship.

The question for me, as a representative of an American Catholic university and as a priest, has been how to deal with this complexity. On my first trip I had mixed feelings. I was deeply moved by the piety and fervor of Chinese worship in the aboveground church, but I was perplexed by the difficult role of the local bishops. Since that visit I have spoken with several Vatican cardinals and other church leaders in the West who seem to have the same ambivalence I do. It is important to keep good relations with the whole Church in China, in the hope that things will improve someday. On the other hand, no one wants to offend the church of the martyrs as though their heroic sacrifice were unimportant.

The underground church considers the aboveground church to be evil and a tool of the government, and there is no doubt that this has sometimes been the case. But it is said that the vast majority of aboveground Catholics have great affection for the Pope and would like union. The problem is the Chinese government.

Shanghai is generally regarded as more dynamic, more relaxed, and more Western than Beijing and most of China. I was absolutely amazed at the scale of development I encountered there. Not only was the downtown one big building project of offices and hotels, but the suburbs looked like suburban D.C., Chicago, or Los Angeles when the boom began in the late 1940s and early 1950s.

During a visit to a Shanghai convent and novitiate for religious women, I celebrated Mass in English for a congregation of about 150 sisters, one of whom translated my brief homily into Chinese. The sisters wore a moderate-style habit, and the head nuns were in their thirties. The convent/novitiate was an old building divided into an infirmary, a sewing room, a dining area, a kitchen, and so on. There was no heat, and we could see our breath indoors. No one could accuse these sisters of living high on the hog.

I met a number of older and infirm sisters from a variety of religious communities, many of whom had been through the times of persecution. Their simple rooms were full of holy pictures and icons, and several wore medals and scapulars. They seemed relatively happy to be together in a community of faith in the latter days of their lives. The young sisters mentioned the inspiration the older religious gave them, and all of us were touched by these women who were pursuing a vocation or living in retirement in a cultural situation where much was uncertain and the past was full of sacrifice and public scorn.

SOUTH KOREA

Korea is a country prominent in the memories of my early teens, when I used to read Sergeant Joe Young comic books that offered an American heroic view of the Korean War—kind of like a John Wayne or Rambo version of Vietnam. Some of the place names on Korea's map evoke famous battles of that war—Pusan, Incheon, and Kwangju, as well as Pyongyang in the North and the Yalu River on the border with China. I remember well General Douglas MacArthur being called back from Korea and retired from service by President Harry Truman. His welcome in Washington was the greatest parade I had ever seen up to that point.

When I first visited Seoul in 1994, the American Embassy was highly fortified, with seven or eight busloads of Korean riot police on standby outside it. The day before my visit, there had been a rumor of a major protest; though it never materialized, the police were there just in case.

No one I met in South Korea on that trip had been in the North since the war. The conservative elements in the government wanted no concessions toward the North in a movement toward unity. Public opinion, on the other hand, favored some concessions, and there was a deep desire to be one country again.

A later visit to South Korea in 2000 coincided with anti-American demonstrations precipitated by a toxic spill in a major river, some acts of U.S. misconduct, and the sheer size of the American military presence. I also found a general optimism in the wake of the first tentative steps toward reunification with North Korea.

INDIA

"I write this entry at 3:50 A.M. sitting in the domestic terminal of the Bombay airport." So reads a journal entry I made during a 1992 visit to India. It continues: "Mosquitoes are hovering, and the temperature is around

60 degrees. When the counter opens at 4:00 A.M., I learn that I should be back at the international terminal, where I just flew in from Frankfurt. Bad advice from one of the stewardesses. Nothing like a little adventure.

"It is only a twenty-minute drive to the other terminal at this hour of the morning, but the driver rips me off and there is an endless supply of baggage carriers and others looking for money and claiming to know a secret way into the airport. I am in India to participate in a meeting of the board of the International Federation of Catholic Universities (IFCU), an important organization on behalf of Catholic higher education.

"The Bombay airport is large and functional, but it displays the state of the economy in small touches of incompletion. It is clean but not attractive. Signs are in English and Hindi, and customs agents are numerous. There is much evidence of the famous Indian adaptation of the British bureaucracy—supervisors looking over the shoulders of ranks of people and an oversupply of aides. Women in saris with a red dot on their foreheads and a small ring in one nostril work the check-in desks along with the men in uniforms. International airports in Third World countries are like havens. They provide a sense of normalcy for travelers from the West, but once you leave their security everything has a touch of the unknown."

That visit to India proved to be full of touches of the unknown. Bombay, for instance, had a distinctive smell that combined an earthiness with a tinge of incense. The Indian racial appearance was as diverse as the stock out of which that heterogeneous nation sprang, and skin color went from light to very dark. I saw straight hair, curls, and Afro-style, and mustaches were common. Three-wheeled vehicles seemed to be the replacement for the former human-powered form of transportation.

My flight from Bombay to Trivandrum gave me a clear view of the Indian Ocean and the coastline that runs straight south. The flight was followed by a three-hour cab ride to Changanacherry, where the IFCU board meeting was hosted by Saint Berchman's College. I do not know if I have the words to describe the cab ride. The first principle was maximum speed no matter who was contending for space on the road. The second principle was to use the horn more than the brake. The third principle was: no contact, no sweat. *My* first and only principle was to say a prayer for safety and not worry.

The ride was a constant bombardment of impressions. Kerala is the most densely populated state in all of India, and people were everywhere—on the roads, in the fields, in small towns, in shops, waiting for buses. Men wore a kind of short skirt tucked around their waist called a *lunghi;* most were shirtless, a few had pants. Women wore brightly colored saris. Thongs were popular as footwear for both sexes. The main road was full of buses, trucks, cabs, cars, motorbikes, bicycles, covered three-wheelers, oxen-driven carts, herds of cows, and even groups of children. Among the sights were old men on their haunches, oblivious to the passing scene; cheap transportation stuffed with people and goods (but no one on the roofs); men urinating into the fields facing away from the road; a little girl skipping along singing to herself.

Kerala State traces its Christian roots back to the apostle Thomas, who is said to have preached to some Jewish communities in the area. Goa, off the west coast, was settled by the Portuguese in the sixteenth century and was a stopping-off point on the way to China and Japan; Saint Francis Xavier, the great Jesuit missionary, is buried there. Kerala is the most Catholic region of India, so it is ironic that for many years the government was Communist. The Communist Party is still one of the largest political parties.

Poverty, pervasive and persistent, is a given in India, yet in Kerala State, with the crowds and activity, it seemed hardly noteworthy. From my hotel window I could see a number of other hotels, presumably catering to businesspeople and tourists. I saw no beggars on the streets, like the infamous scenes of Calcutta, and the markets displayed abundant food.

A group excursion along the waterways of Kerala turned into one of those adrenalin-rush sorts of international experiences that make traveling long distances worthwhile and leave you supersaturated with images and impressions about a new place and a people different from yourself. The two-level boat, which just fit our group of thirty, was flat-bottomed and motorized, and most of the seats were down below, only a couple of feet above the water. We passed people everywhere, including women doing the wash by banging the clothes on rocks at the side of the canal, and others cleaning the clothes on their backs by taking a dip. Several times I saw advertisements in English for washing soap and detergent on the walls behind the washerwomen: "Sunspot soap. For clean clothes."

Little kids were taking baths and young men were swimming in the canal, even though it is both the common sewer and the region's water source. Long canoe-like boats carried people or goods, and an occasional fisherman occupied a boat by himself. One vessel was a floating pawn shop. The bigger boats had motors, while the less elaborate ones were propelled by long poles. Small children waved to us and flashed big smiles. Adults were more quizzical; it was we who were the sideshow for them. I thought several times of Vietnam War movie scenes, only here no one was shooting at us; we were tourists taking in the scene, not a patrol boat.

The Kurisumala Ashram is at the opposite end of Kerala, on the west slopes of the Ghats Mountains. In 1958, a Trappist monk named Father Francis Mayeux came to that part of India to brush up on his Sanskrit. He was still there thirty-four years later. Going by the name Father Francis Scharya, he founded a retreat community (an ashram) even before the land became accessible by road and while leopards, cheetahs, wild boars, and monkeys still roamed the region. Father Scharya, who resembled a classic Indian guru with a long beard, monastic robes, and wizened face, greeted us warmly and told us his story. Because the soil was too poor to grow tea, the landowner donated it to the monastery. The purpose of the ashram is to be a center of prayer for a community of twenty male monks who work the land, provide hospitality for spiritual pilgrims, and pray.

Kerala, in religious terms, is like Ireland or parts of Italy or Spain. Evidence of Catholic piety and devotion is everywhere, and one sees numerous churches, schools, convents, meeting halls, statues, crosses, and religious pictures. All the local clergy and religious are native-born, and there is a surplus of them; as a result, many clergy and religious from Kerala are missionaries in other parts of the world. On my trip back from the ashram, we stopped at a shrine to Blessed Sister Alphonsa (1910–46), who founded a religious community. During Pope John Paul II's 1986 visit to India, he declared her Blessed.

I wonder whether India can hold together as a nation. Can the notion of India unify all the religious, cultural, and regional differences? That, of course, was Gandhi's dream. Infrastructure problems are immense. Money aside, where do you put the roads, parks, airports, and train lines when people are already everywhere? It is said that one hundred million Indians, or 11 percent of the population, are middle class—which is quite an achievement—and there is also a small upper class. Yet most people are poor, and there is a great hunger for education. The great ministries of the Catholic Church in India are education and health care. Christians are in the forefront of the women's movement, and leadership is particularly strong among Indian women religious. Yet this may be one of the things Muslim and Hindu fundamentalists find most offensive about Christians.

INDONESIA

Indonesia, when I stopped there in the summer of 1988, was the fifth largest country in the world, and demographers were predicting that it would surpass the United States in population. It is an archipelago made up of 13,677 islands; the five main islands are Sumatra, Java, Kalimantan, Sulawesi, and Irian Jaya. A majority of the population lives on the island of Java, where Jakarta, the capital, is located. The island of Bali is Indonesia's most fabled tourist attraction.

Indonesia's national philosophy is *Pancasila*—an attempt to carve out unity amid great cultural and geographical diversity based on five principles: belief in the one and only God; a just and civilized humanity; the unity of Indonesia; democracy guided by inner wisdom; and social justice for all the people of Indonesia. The word for "God" is not Allah, because that would be Islamic, but a word similar to "lordship." *Pancasila* tells more about what the national philosophy is not than what it is. It is not acceptable to be not religious, for example, since then it is presumed that one is a Communist and therefore an enemy of the state—an attitude influenced by the 1965 Communist struggle in Indonesia.

Catholicism came to Indonesia 450 years ago, and Saint Francis Xavier was the most famous early missioner. The Portuguese and later the Dutch were the primary evangelizers. The Japanese occupation in World War II was a real setback to Catholicism, and persecution produced a number of martyrs. In 1961, Pope John XXIII established a Catholic hierarchy in Indonesia, signifying its ability to function as a nonmission church.

Some impressions of Jakarta: a narrow street with numerous small shops all devoted to men with Singer sewing machines fashioning seat covers for autos; vendors in tiny stands selling food atop flowing sewers; batik shirts worn outside the pants even in formal settings; pictures of President Suharto displayed in prominent places. The people display a variety of racial stocks, and smiles spring readily to their faces.

Taman Mini is a park on the scale of Disneyland that attempts to recreate the cultural diversity of Indonesia in buildings, museums, artifacts, film, and flora and fauna. The central museum contains four floors of displays of the dress, arts, and traditions of the different provinces. Taman Mini was a highlight for me, and I recommend it to anyone journeying to Jakarta. Yet one can't help wondering whether the expenditure of large sums of money for such purposes in a developing country reflects the right priority.

In Bali, everything was lush, green, bright, and clean. The population was 90 percent Hindu, and religion seemed to be genuine and pervasive in the life of the average person. There were elaborate temples in each village, and shrines with votive offerings of food and flowers in most of the homes; it was like statues to the Blessed Mother, crucifixes, or Infant of Prague replicas. Public religious devotions and festivals were integrated into the rhythm of life.

We watched a performance of a Hindu folktale set to dance and music; it was a bit too commercial for my taste, with all the tourists taking photographs.

My favorite spot on Bali was a Hindu temple at a point where springs come out of the mountain; it was serene and well kept up, with some people taking a ritual bath. Bali is a beautiful island that has much to recommend it to a visitor—a natural charm, friendly people, and a pleasant climate all year long.

TIBET

During a trip to China in 1987, I flew from Chengdu, capital of Szechwan Province, to Lhasa in Tibet. The flight took us over the Himalayas, the world's highest mountain chain, and from the air we could see settlements in the valleys and along the rivers, all in seemingly impossible terrain. One of the rivers, on the border of China and Tibet, was the site of a famous battle in 1948 in the war between Chiang Kai-Shek and the Red Army.

The Lhasa airport was a major base for the Chinese air force, with three helicopters, twelve jet fighters, and armed soldiers all around the perimeter. Clearly, the Chinese military occupation was a fact of life. The ride from the airport to Lhasa was along a paved road beside a river, and the overall effect was like Lake Titicaca in the altiplano of Peru and Bolivia. The typical Tibetan settlement seemed to be a compound of houses with a large walled-in open area, where I'm sure animals were kept.

Long wooden poles with multicolored small flags attached were clumped together in various places—at waterfalls, on precipices, atop houses.

Our hotel was a brand-new Holiday Inn with rooms for about two hundred guests—it struck me as incongruous to be pampered in a Holiday Inn in one of the most forbidding countries in the world, a place that just seven years earlier the *National Geographic* recommended that tourists avoid unless they were prepared to really rough it.

Lhasa sits at about 12,000 feet and averages only 18 inches of rain a year, most of it falling in the summer as an offshoot of monsoons farther south. The climate is generally sunny with moderate temperatures, although north of Tibet there is some of the worst weather in the world. A walk through one of the side streets reminded me of a barrio neighborhood in Latin America—open sewage, garbage, simply constructed houses, a smell in the air. But the people were extremely friendly.

Buddhism was introduced into Tibet from India, and despite the Chinese takeover in 1951, many consider Tibet still to be the most religious nation on earth. The Dalai Lama was proclaimed to be an incarnation of the deity beginning with the fifth Dalai in the Middle Ages. The present Dalai fled to India with sixty thousand of his followers in the 1950s, but he is still highly regarded in Tibet.

The Potala, built up the side of a cliff and considered one of the architectural wonders of the world, is the central symbol of Lhasa. It served as the home of the Dalai Lama and his monks, as a burial ground, and as a meeting place. The best way to describe it is to say it would be an ideal spot for a game of hide-and-seek; it's an endless maze of altars, small rooms, ladders, passageways, and courtyards. Within it were Buddhas in all shapes and configurations, usually attended by a monk and sometimes by his young son. There were candles burning in otherwise dim rooms and numerous native stands with yak butter— the smell doesn't exactly reek, but it is pungent and relatively unpleasant to the Western nose. Great artistry went into the statues and the surrounding multicolored images and stories on the wooden walls and ceilings. A fair number of devotees were chanting prayers or making offerings, and there was a genuine religious sense. Chinese soldiers could be found among the tourists.

Celebrating Mass in this part of the world had some special dimensions for me, since it could well have been the only Mass said in that whole country on a given day. God is surely present to the people here, but in a way much different from our own.

Our party toured the Drepung Monastery, which once held the largest concentration of Buddhist monks in the world. Today it is a fully functioning place of worship with about two hundred resident monks. It is hard to describe the effect of the place, stuck dramatically in a mountainside with peaks up above. There too the prevalent smell was of yak butter, contributed by worshipers who made the rounds of the various shrines, putting in some yak butter, offering money, and prostrating themselves on the ground.

The shrines were dimly lighted with candles, and this tended to accentuate the yellow visage of the Buddhas.

There must have been several thousand Buddha figures, the largest of them two or three times life-size. Some were grotesquely shaped, like evil monsters. At one point there was a large stone about four feet in diameter which each person circled about ten times while banging a small rock against it. I was not sure what the ritual signified.

Hundreds of Tibetan worshipers were present. Most were families, everyone from infants to grandparents. They were joyous and friendly and not at all distracted by our presence. This monastery was built in the 1400s, but unlike many European cathedrals of the same vintage, it is not a museum or a mausoleum; the living faith of the people is manifest. The monks were robed simply and had shaved heads; they were of all ages, and the young ones liked to be photographed. They eat mashed potatoes and yak meat and drink tea and beer. I didn't feel any great call to sign up.

My impression of Tibet was that the Chinese see the country primarily as a buffer zone between themselves and India. Although they have made some improvements in the economy, there is little evidence of any grand strategy for social change. The Tibetans, on the other hand, are survivors and probably leave it all in the hands of God (or of the Dalai Lama, if he should ever return).

VIETNAM

In the summer of 2002, I paid my first visit to Vietnam, a country that is closely connected to my memories of the 1960s and beyond. I lost ten to fifteen Notre Dame classmates in that war, mostly helicopter pilots, and I took part in the march on the Pentagon (made famous by Norman Mailer's *Armies of the Night*). That turned out to be my last march; when I read many of the banners I found I had no sympathy for the rationales they expressed for American disengagement. I have been to the Vietnam Memorial in D.C. more times than I can count, and each time I have been moved by the low-lying black stone with the names listed in sequence of their deaths.

Who from my generation doesn't feel as though he or she was already in Vietnam? We have seen *Apocalypse Now, The Deer Hunter, Full Metal Jacket, Born on the Fourth of July, Platoon,* and many more movies, not to mention the memoirs and the novels. We remember the endless newsreel footage of that era, and the public protests and the progressively more contentious commentary. We learned of unpopular officers being "fragged" and of R&R in Thailand and of the secret bombing of Cambodia and Laos. We remember Presidents Kennedy and Johnson and Nixon, and General Westmoreland and John McNamara and Henry Kissinger. We remember the Tet Offensive and Cam Ranh Bay and the Mekong Delta and the Hanoi Hilton and Da Nang air base and the evacuation of the U.S. Embassy in Saigon. There was Agent Orange and carpet bombing and body counts and My Lai and helicopter rescues and enemy troops emerging from underground caves. The loss of life on both sides was horrendous, yet after we pulled out, Vietnam went on to fight China in the north and to invade Cambodia—until Vietnam too returned home after defeat on a foreign soil.

As my flight landed at the Saigon (Ho Chi Minh City) airport, there were manned watchtowers every 100 yards or so. About a third of the people on our plane were Caucasians, and sitting behind me was a former American soldier back for the first time since the end of the war. Father Martin Nguyen, C.S.C., met my group at the airport. The passport control guy was a little surly, but I find they usually are in Communist countries.

Saigon preserves some French influence, especially in the older neighborhoods. The streets reminded me of beehives or an ant nest. The common vehicle is the motor scooter, and people of all ages and conditions were riding them. Bicycles flowed in and out of traffic in parallel and congruent streams, sometimes five abreast. Some bikes had whole families on them, and a few had major appliances strapped on the rider's back. At some intersections they crossed at perpendicular angles, and it was a wonder of nature that they made it through.

We visited the War Remnants Museum, which includes an outdoor display of captured American tanks, planes, guns, and other paraphernalia, and a series of indoor displays with a heavy propagandistic tone. One entire room contained war photographs, and another showed victims of bombing or bacteriological or chemical agents. Ironically, the museum's visitors included a mix of Americans and Vietnamese, and there was little tension between them.

On the way to the Saigon airport early one morning, we saw a fair number of people out doing their morning exercises. Some elderly men and women were doing a kind of Asian calisthenics, and others were walking or jogging. Because I didn't see any fat people, I concluded it couldn't be for reasons of weight control. Perhaps the Party encourages physical fitness.

From Saigon we flew to Hue, on the thin strip of Vietnam between the South China Sea and Laos. It has mountains near the coast, like parts of California, and is about a two-hour drive south of the DMZ, the old border between North and South Vietnam. During the war many of Hue's buildings were destroyed three or four times. Although the city is a Buddhist center, there is a thriving Catholic community there as well—but "stalwart" and "faithful" are probably better words than "thriving," because it is hard to thrive under a Communist regime.

We stopped at the Convent of the Holy Cross Sisters on the Feast of Saint Thomas the Apostle, and Martin celebrated Mass for a group of eight sisters. After Communion they sang a beautiful Vietnamese hymn, and when Mass was done we sat around and sipped a cold drink together. I told them our priorities on this trip to Vietnam—to visit the sisters first and then the bishop— and they liked our perspective. Their community runs a kindergarten for poor young boys from the North and also provides living accommodations for high school girls. About fifteen sisters were preparing to make their final vows soon.

We paid a visit to Archbishop Nguyen Nhu The, who told us there are fifty thousand Catholics in Hue in a population of two million. He has about fifty active priests, a few of whom have studied in France, but none, so far, in the United States. Relations with the local Buddhists are delicate, he said, and there is more cooperation in concrete deeds of service than in official parleys. At lunch we joined seven priests who were awaiting government approval before they could go to their assigned churches—such is life under the Communists. The meal was quite good— rice, fish, chicken, meat, bread, and palm-nut dessert. I think they had a feast because we were there.

We took a driving tour around Hue. A walled fortress right off the Perfume River with a moat around it was the scene of some violent fighting during the war, and five or six American tanks and half-tracks are now on display there, presumably to suggest that the Vietcong bested a powerful military force. A giant Vietnamese flag flew in the center—a yellow star on a light red backdrop.

Never in my wildest dreams did I imagine that I would spend an Independence Day in Hanoi, the center of the Vietcong's effort to seize control of the South, and the headquarters of Ho Chi Minh. North Vietnam was also the location of Dien Bien Phu, the French fortress that the Vietcong seized in the 1950s, forcing France to pull out. Dr. Tom Dooley, a Notre Dame graduate and Navy doctor, was involved in some of the early medical-support operations near the DMZ. His letter back to Father Hesburgh appears next to the kneelers at our Grotto.

The U.S. Embassy was throwing an invitation-only bash in a large modern hotel to celebrate the Fourth of July. We arrived just as the Marine Color Guard was marching in to band accompaniment. I would say there were five hundred people there, including the diplomatic corps, the staff from the embassy, businesspeople, and representatives from the Vietnamese government. Along the sides of the grand ballroom was food galore, including hamburgers and hot dogs. Waitresses walked around with trays of water, soft drinks, beer, wine, and champagne. Red, white, and, blue banners festooned the upper walls along with American insignias and USA signs. Who would have thought it?

Ambassador Raymond Burghardt gave a talk appropriate for the occasion, and the Finance Minister of Vietnam responded. Then there were toasts. Ambassador Burghardt spent time in Vietnam during the war and is fluent in Vietnamese, Mandarin Chinese, and Spanish. It would be nice if we had more ambassadors with that kind of credentials. We met two Notre Dame grads at the reception. One was the co-director of Vietnam Assistance for the Handicapped; he is confined to a wheelchair, having been injured near Hue in 1968.

During our visit we kept hearing that the States were on high alert lest there be terrorist attacks on July 4. How ironic that we could be safer in Hanoi than we might be at home.

SNAPSHOTS

PRESIDENT GEORGE H. W. BUSH
AT CAMP DAVID

Having grown up in the Washington, D.C., area, I've always had a fascination with Camp David. Although the presidential retreat was referred to frequently in the media, there was never any specific information about its location. In my imagination it was more like the headquarters of the Wizard of Oz than a simple rural retreat.

I finally had a chance to see Camp David firsthand when President George H. W. Bush and his wife, Barbara, invited the founding members of the Points of Light Foundation there for a strategizing session. Buses carried our group from a D.C. hotel into the Catoctin Mountains of western Maryland, between Frederick and the Gettysburg battle site. Camp David was staffed by Navy enlisted personnel and surrounded by two high barbed-wire fences controlled by Marine security. We were greeted at the entrance by Secret Service agents, who inspected the undercarriage of the buses. After leaving the buses, we went through an airport-style security gate. Once inside the camp, things changed to a much more relaxed mode.

It quickly became clear to me why so many presidential families enjoy spending weekends at Camp David. They can wear what they want, there are no press asking embarrassing questions, and there are plenty of opportunities for recreation and leisure. The buildings are chalet style, reminding one of a fairly well-to-do camp in Colorado.

After being greeted by President and Mrs. Bush, we were ushered into the equivalent of the Cabinet Room, where our group held a discussion session with the President. The Points of Light Foundation is a nonpartisan group of American leaders committed to promoting volunteer service across every dimension of American public life, and the board members who were at Camp David were of every political stripe and had varying degrees of experience in the movement.

During our deliberations, the two Bush dogs scurried around the room, sometimes pursuing each other under the long table. At lunch I ended up at Mrs. Bush's table and found her to be a wonderful and engaging host. After the meal, the President took us to us his office-away-from-the-office. Along the way he pointed out, with a gleam in his eye, a target-practice paper form that hung on the wall outside the office. It had a couple of bullet holes in it, and on the top of the form were the names "Bush" and another Spanish name. The President informed us it had been seized from Panama President Manuel Noriega's headquarters after American troops raided that country. It seems that Noriega had been using the form for target practice.

Before we left the compound, we visited the Camp David gift shop. There was great enthusiasm among my colleagues to take home some memento of the visit. Since I don't have the shopping gene, I was reluctant to go along, but when I saw how avidly how the others were buying souvenirs, I decided to buy a couple of plates for my two sisters.

President George H. W. Bush, Commencement 1992

Notre Dame invited President George H. W. Bush to be our commencement speaker in our sesquicentennial year, 1992, and he readily agreed. The planning for a presidential visit involves complicated logistics, with a lot of Secret Service advance work. Our campus security and event planners always do a great job, however, and problems are usually at a minimum. On the morning of the commencement ceremonies, I was driven to the South Bend airport to await the arrival of Air Force One. Once the President landed and was properly greeted, the two of us got into the presidential limousine for the escorted ride to the campus. The President was rather apologetic about the heavy security and explained that it is an inevitable part of contemporary American life. I remembered from an earlier visit he made to the campus for a football game when he was Vice President that he seemed reluctant to accept the orders of the Secret Service regarding how much time he could spend on the field before the pregame flag ceremony. He commented then that if the Secret Service always had their way he would have no freedom of movement at all, and that goes against the grain of any politician.

It's a relatively brief ride from the airport to our campus, and when you're going by way of a section of Indiana toll road that's been closed to traffic, with police cars at every overpass, it's even briefer than usual. During the ride, the President described an incident that made a point about the need for security. He said he and his wife sometimes liked to get away from the White House and go unannounced to a local restaurant. They were frequenting one restaurant in the Virginia suburbs across the river from Washington when someone spotted this trend and began coming to that restaurant armed. On one of his visits to the restaurant, the Secret Service was able to spot and arrest the person. Thus the difficulty of doing anything spontaneous when you are President of the United States.

As most people who have watched presidential caravans know, there are always two limos, either of which could be carrying the President. Often the first limo is a dummy with nobody but the driver in it. When President Ronald Reagan visited the campus, he pointed out that one way to have fun on such trips was to watch people waving at the first limo; then as the real one passed he'd point and they would be discombobulated because they couldn't recover fast enough to resume waving. President Bush made the same point and seemed to derive equal fun from the game.

The commencement speech went well, and the assembled graduates and family members and faculty were pleased that the President of the United States chose to be with us.

President George W. Bush, Commencement 2001

Growing up in Washington, D.C., I developed a fundamental respect for the American system of government and for those entrusted by election (or in the case of the Supreme Court, by appointment and approval) with responsibility for leadership. Along the way I have met a few charlatans, demagogues, and people lacking in character, but overall I have been impressed by how these individuals try to negotiate the complicated give-and-take of political life with integrity and hard work. All of this is to say that I have tried to work within the system myself, as an educational leader and representative of Notre Dame. I have a party preference, strong opinions about some issues, and a concern about the moral foundation of government, yet in most cases I seek for common ground and try to establish some rapport with those who have been duly elected.

George W. Bush had been to Notre Dame on three occasions before his commencement visit in 2001, two of them for football games. When he hosted our women's championship basketball team at the White House, along with the Duke men's team, I was part of the official party. On a bright, warm, sunny afternoon, with the teams lined up in the Rose Garden and the rest of us seated on folding chairs facing the teams and the White House itself, President Bush appeared from the Oval Office at the exact time assigned and said some words of greeting. He quoted Coach Muffet McGraw's son and made some humorous comments about his reputation as a mangler of vocabulary.

Then he invited the two teams and their working staffs, presidents, and athletic directors to spend some time in the Oval Office, where he offered historical background about the room and its furnishings. He made special mention of one of the paintings on the wall that had been loaned by Joe and Jan O'Neill (Joe is a Notre Dame alumnus and a longtime family friend of the Bushes). The President was warm and friendly and quite welcoming of the young people. I noticed that Shane Battier, the Duke star and an Academic All-American, hit it off well with our Ruth Riley. In fact, the two teams seemed quite similar in the personal qualities of the players.

At the end of our time in the Oval Office, President Bush wished us well, and the two groups continued a tour of the rest of the White House. Along the way the President told me he was looking forward to coming to our campus for commencement, and I heard him commenting to some non–Notre Dame people about the beauty of the campus. That visit to the White House was my first personal interaction with George W. Bush.

I am sometimes asked how we go about choosing a commencement speaker and how, in the case of a President, we are able to get an affirmative answer. The process begins with discussions within the University administration. In the modern era, Presidents Eisenhower, Carter, Reagan, and the senior Bush have all spoken at commencements, and when George W. Bush was finally ruled the winner of the 2000 election I sent him a letter of invitation. We then began to mobilize various friends of Notre Dame who might have some influence in the new administration. In the end, it was the personal request of Joe O'Neill, the man who first introduced George and Laura Bush to each other, that carried the day. There was some time lag before we could announce it publicly, but we knew with a high degree of reliability (barring some international crisis) that the new President would be our commencement speaker. The other two schools where he would speak that year were Yale University (his alma mater) and the Naval Academy.

Preparation for the visit began weeks ahead of time and involved both the Secret Service and the presidential staff. Because we have been hosts to many heads of state through the years, our campus group was well prepared. Once the speaker was identified, the demand for commencement tickets went up—for example, a record group of trustees decided to attend the ceremony, and the White House media also were allotted several rows of seats.

Before Air Force One landed, knots of people already were gathering along the highways. At the airport everything was abuzz. We pulled up to a large hangar, where a Secret Service agent let me in without checking me out in any way. The hangar was empty but the airport side was open, and I could see the police motorcycles, police cars, Secret Service vans, and the presidential limo. Straight in front of me was the portable staircase for Air Force One. Flying overhead was a helicopter checking out the plane's approach route.

Finally I saw Air Force One on the glide path—a Boeing 747 less than two years old and carrying every protective and communication gadget available. What amazed me was that, despite its size, it came to a stop faster than our small University plane does; it is specially designed to land and take off from short runways. When the President and Mrs. Bush appeared at the top of the stairway and descended, followed by various aides and Condoleezza Rice, the crowd cheered. In the limo the Bushes sat facing forward and I sat in a jump seat facing the rear, in front of the President. The limo was shorter than some I have been in, so our knees knocked together until we found the right spacing.

The President was intent on waving to people along our travel route. Since most of them were on his wife's side of the car, he had to lean forward and stretch a bit. Four or five motorcycles led our caravan, with a mix of police cars and Secret Service vans front and rear, and every overpass had a police car on it. The limo conversation revolved around the welcome I was sure the President would receive and the arrival ceremony at the Joyce Athletic and Convocation Center, where the commencement exercises were to be held and where the Bushes would be introduced to a young Mexican-American student from Texas who had won the Laura Bush Scholarship.

You cannot let yourself out of the presidential limo from the inside—the Secret Service needs to check the scene first. When the limo doors were opened, I had to scrunch my legs to get past the President's knees and lead the way. After we entered the service passageway into the Joyce Center, a large movable metal barrier was closed behind us. With the security contingent, we went immediately to the men's basketball locker room for introductions, picture taking, and conversation. After five or ten minutes everyone was escorted out of the room except for Mr. and Mrs. Bush, Condi Rice, Jan O'Neill, and me. We sat down on a couple of sofas facing each other. In a few minutes Joe O'Neill came back, and we needed to bring over another small sofa, so the President and I ended up pushing it across the room.

The Bushes and the O'Neills clearly have a close and comfortable relationship. We talked about the visit, about the President's other visits to Notre Dame for football games, and about the trip he would make to Yale University after leaving South Bend. I think it is fair to say that he expected a different kind of welcome at Yale and seemed a bit anxious about that trip. When the President at one point went off to the restroom in the locker area, he was preceded by two agents, even though there was no other access point into the room and the whole area had been checked thoroughly before we arrived—talk about a trip to the john being a big deal. I went later myself, to much less fanfare.

Finally we went upstairs to a pre-commencement luncheon in the Monogram Room, which was so crowded that it was difficult for the staff to serve the meal. The President was on my left, the First Lady on my right. About five minutes into the meal, people began to come over to the dais, purportedly to say hello to me but really to meet the President and have their picture taken. At first it was okay, but then people became bolder and it became quite congested in front of us. I could see that the Secret Service were not happy, so I finally stood up and asked people to move away.

President Bush did not eat much, and neither did I. The big difference between us was that a Secret Service agent brought out his food and drink separately and took it back afterward. I asked about the second step, and he said it's the only way to determine what happened if a problem arises. During the meal, I chatted with both of our guests, but more with the President than the First Lady. At one point, Science Dean Frank Castellino came by and we talked about stem-cell research. The President made reference to some hard lobbying by the American Catholic bishops in opposition to government support of such research. I discussed some education-related issues with Mrs. Bush, and at one point she asked me to send her the bibliography for the seminar course I teach.

After the meal, the Bushes and I went to a large office that served as a holding area. Because the start of commencement was slightly delayed, we were there about twenty-five or thirty minutes, during which the President called back to Washington and talked with his Chief of Staff about media coverage of the energy issue. He also watched a videotaped digest of television coverage of his activities the previous day. Then he turned on a Cubs baseball game without the sound. He kidded his wife when she made uninformed comments about various baseball players.

When the time came to line up for the ceremony, there was plenty of security. The President spoke comforting, encouraging words to our valedictorian and had his picture taken with the student who was to say the opening prayer, an architecture graduate who wore an image of the White House atop his mortarboard.

The commencement exercises took about two hours, and the consensus was that President Bush gave an excellent talk. Its theme was the proper response to the

problem of poverty, and the responsibilities of government, corporations, religious groups, and individuals. He
connected the theme to his push for faith-based initiatives
and used as an example Notre Dame's involvement in the
South Bend Center for the Homeless.

There had been speculation about whether anyone
would try to disrupt the ceremony. An odd mix of protes-
tors (many having no connection to Notre Dame) exercised
their constitutional prerogatives by gathering outside.
Neither President Bush nor I ever saw them, but afterward
the media gave them some attention. Inside, some of the
graduates and faculty chose to wear one ribbon or another
pinned to their gowns to indicate support for or opposition to several causes. As far as I know, only one graduate
during the talk faced away from the stage, and he prayed
the rosary during President Bush's talk. The President
read his speech effectively, using the teleprompter device
comfortably and establishing good rapport with his audience. The next day at Yale, he looked more on edge.

I found the President relaxed, down-to-earth, and unpre-
tentious. He did not mangle the English language in my company. He was kind to everyone with whom he interacted,
and patient with autograph requests and picture taking.
I believe he genuinely enjoyed his time at Notre Dame.

DONALD TRUMP AND RAY CHAMBERS

For one of my many trips to New York City, Hank
McCormack, Notre Dame's regional director of devel-

opment in the New York area, scheduled fund-raising meetings for me with two business executives: Donald Trump and Ray Chambers. In my hotel room the night before, I read a chapter from Donald Trump's book in which he mentioned how much he had enjoyed being invited to the rectory at Saint Patrick's Cathedral for a meal with Cardinal O'Connor. I took this to imply that he had some unpublicized interest in matters of religion, although I knew him only from his reputation as a playboy extraordinaire, a flamboyant entrepreneur, and a glutton for publicity.

The following day, Hank and I made our way to the Trump Tower, where we had been told to take the private elevator right up to his office. At the foot of the elevator were perhaps a hundred copies of the book. Mr. Trump welcomed us into his office and we sat in chairs on opposite sides of his uncluttered desk. He was handsome and expensively dressed and extremely self-confident. During the course of our half-hour together, his secretary came in six or seven times with messages, which he spread one by one across his desk. This seemed to communicate to us the not-so-subtle message that the world was awaiting his return to availability. I kept searching for common ground, either about higher education or religion—or something. All we learned was that his chief lawyer had a son interested in coming to Notre Dame and that that was the main reason he had been open to meeting with us. As the meeting went on, it was clear to me that our session was going nowhere as far as fund-raising was concerned. At one point he said, "I have not yet reached my philanthropic period." I figured that about summed it up.

As a parting gesture, he offered to sign a copy of his book for me. Feeling that I had just been in a Soviet–U.S. type of negotiation, I responded by offering to sign a copy of the book about Notre Dame that I had brought for him. Like two negotiators forging a treaty of détente, we exchanged books.

The next appointment was with Ray Chambers, who also had no known Notre Dame connection but, like Donald Trump, was a successful businessperson. At the top of a high-rise in downtown Manhattan, we were quickly ushered into his office. Mr. Chambers is approximately the same age as Trump but entirely opposite in personality. We were joined by Vince Naimoli, a Notre Dame graduate and a successful businessperson in his own right. With a little prodding, Mr. Chambers described his intention to use the bulk of his money to try to make a difference in the quality of life for inner-city youth in New Jersey. He told us he had pledged to provide full tuition support for any graduate of a specific grade school who made it into college. In addition, it turned out that he was involved in a number of other projects to help young people. All this he told us humbly and unabashedly, with a sense of real commitment to the needs of others.

Since that initial conversation I have been involved with Ray Chambers on a number of national activities, including the Points of Light Foundation. Later he became a member of the Notre Dame Board of Trustees and an honorary degree recipient.

Those two meetings could not have been more enlightening insofar as the contrast they provided. It wasn't so much a matter of one being a villain and another being a hero, but rather two different perspectives about the responsibilities of those with great means.

MARTIN LUTHER KING JR.

Although I never met Martin Luther King Jr., my life did intersect his in a significant way. In 1963 my father was part of the planning committee for the famous March on Washington; his role was to provide hospitality and encourage participation from the Catholic community. I was very proud of my father for doing that, since the pre-march rumors included predictions of an urban bloodbath.

On the day of the march, we arrived early and with some trepidation at the Mall area, between the Washington Monument and the Lincoln Memorial. The crowds were orderly, and many people were well dressed, reflecting a well-planned effort to squelch fears and foster positive feelings about the event. Over a loudspeaker system, Peter, Paul and Mary and other music groups of the time were singing the songs of the civil rights movement. By the time the speechmaking began on the steps of the Lincoln Memorial, I was already amazed at both the tranquillity and the power of the event. Dr. King gave his famous "I Have a Dream" speech that day. It remains one of the great pieces of American oratory, and I always have felt privileged to have been present for its delivery.

Our second connection came in 1968 after Dr. King had been assassinated in Memphis. There was some rioting in Washington, where I was studying at Holy Cross Seminary, but by evening things seemed to have calmed down. The next day another seminarian, who happened to have had battlefield experience in Korea, and I ventured forth by car to survey my native city. I felt confident that I could read signs of trouble and avoid any difficulty.

After touring downtown, I drove over to Fifteenth Street NW and took a right turn on Florida Avenue. Traffic was somewhat backed up, so I turned onto Fourteenth Street—where all hell broke loose. Hundreds of people were throwing rocks and bottles and looting stores. The brand-new car I was driving stalled in the middle of the road, and a gigantic rock smashed the windshield, but the safety glass prevented it from breaking all the way through. All the other windows were smashed as well.

By the time I was able to get the car started again, all the other traffic had disappeared out of panic, and I hit almost 70 miles an hour going north. I encountered several other areas of violent activity before turning east to get back to the seminary. When we reached Georgia Avenue, another riot was taking place, but because our car had already been badly damaged we were left alone.

Eventually I made it back to northeast Washington and stopped at the Twelfth Precinct police station. One officer had been left on duty, and his radio was crackling with a city gone mad. I explained what had happened and he asked if anyone was hurt. When I said no, he said, "Get out of here. This city is up for grabs and we can't pay attention to every minor event."

My third significant connection with Dr. King took place many years later, when I was invited by the King family to be one of a number of speakers on Dr. King's birthday at Ebenezer Baptist Church in Atlanta. What a great thrill it was for me to be there with a cross-section of America, in a church that I had known only by reputation. Each of us spoke from our hearts about the impact Dr. King had had on our lives and our country. As is customary in the black religious tradition in America, the congregation responded with amens and other comments as each of us spoke. With sadness I made reference to the continuing discrepancy between the realities of American life and the dreams that Dr. King articulated so eloquently from the steps of the Lincoln Memorial.

Martin Luther King Jr. will be seen in history, I believe, as a great man, who had his share of human flaws but who reminded the nation by his preaching, writing, and example that we still have a long way to go toward realizing the dream of being "one nation under God, . . . with Liberty and Justice for all."

PRESIDENT AND MRS. JIMMY CARTER

Jimmy Carter paid a visit to the Notre Dame campus the year he was running for President. He clearly tried to direct his remarks to a Catholic audience both on campus and nationally. He struck me as thoughtful and bright, and he had a great toothy smile.

Many years later, he and Rosalyn returned to campus to accept the Notre Dame Award, our highest recognition for people in the international arena. The award went to both Carters in celebration of their great spirit of service and commitment in the years following their time in the White House. On the day the Carters arrived, I met the party at the private-aircraft side of the South Bend airport and we divided up among several cars. We of course had the usual Secret Service contingent, yet what struck me most about the ride was that this former President waited at each stoplight and was treated more like a private individual than a former President.

At dinner that evening we had a wonderful conversation about our guests' involvement with Habitat for Humanity and various peacekeeping activities, and about the religious commitment and motivation that underlay all of that. Jimmy Carter spoke about the books he had written, about teaching religion at his local church, and about his desire to be an agent of peacekeeping in various parts of the world.

In his talk at the award ceremony, he spoke eloquently about the connection between his religious convictions and his involvement in projects for human betterment. Several of us had a sense that once the burdens of presidential office were lifted, he was better able to be himself and to find issues worth giving himself over to. Mrs. Carter, of course, had been by his side through all of this. She may not be as visible a public figure, but she is a very impressive person of character and dignity. To my way of thinking, Jimmy and Rosalyn Carter have provided a model well worth emulating. In this day and age, when many Americans live to a ripe old age, it is desirable that our political leaders contribute something substantial for the country and humanity.

PATRICIO AYLWIN, CHILE

During a visit to Chile in 1997 I had an hour-long discussion with former President Patricio Aylwin, who had received an honorary degree from Notre Dame and is a good friend of the University. Because of his role in bringing back democracy to Chile after the Pinochet dictatorship, Aylwin is generally revered in his own country.

When Aylwin became president, he said, he faced two fundamental challenges: telling the truth about the widespread violation of human rights under the Pinochet dictatorship and bringing some degree of justice relative to these violations; and making the economic system compatible with the new democratic order, a task that included raising workers' salaries and trying to eradicate poverty. Referring to a detailed report on the Pinochet years issued by a Commission on Truth and Reconciliation, he said he believed that it was more important to tell the truth than to punish all the offenders.

With regard to the economy, the challenge was to prove that Chile could continue to grow under democracy despite fears in the business community about inflation and his populist policies. Aylwin's regime reformed tax law, developed infrastructure (including one hundred thousand houses for the poor each year), and worked on public services. A recent book, he acknowledged, had been critical of his regime—with Pinochet still in charge of the military, the author claimed, nothing had really changed. But Aylwin was convinced that if he had challenged the military he would not have been able to achieve national reconciliation. If he had to do it all over again, he said, he would choose the same course.

Aylwin criticized the Catholic Church for being too preoccupied with private and sexual morality. He believed that open and sophisticated discussion of public policy matters and priorities is needed. Young people, he lamented, have become too influenced by a U.S. materialist model; they are interested in public service, but their capacity for idealism needs to be promoted.

I was very impressed by President Aylwin. He has the look of a national leader, and he has focused his public career in heroic service to his country.

POPE JOHN PAUL II

During a visit to Rome with Dick Warner, Bill Beauchamp, and Tim Scully in the summer of 1995, we had the privilege of concelebrating Mass with the Holy Father. We were instructed to arrive with alb and stole at the bronze door of Saint Peter's by 6:45 A.M. Around 6:30 we walked from our hotel to Saint Peter's, which looked magnificent at that time of day: The Square was almost empty, the swallows were flying their morning pattern, and a few Swiss guards in full regalia were visible. Despite its mammoth size, Saint Peter's looked roseate and softly appealing.

We reported to the papal apartments' side of the square, where a layman and two Swiss guards checked off our names and led us to an anteroom with about fifteen people in it. Around 6:50 more people arrived, and we walked up several flights of a broad ceremonial staircase and then took two elevators up to the level of the Pope's quarters. Once again we waited—in a large salon with high ceilings and religious art ranging from traditional European style to contemporary African ivory pieces.

At this point the priests among us vested and then joined the laypeople in the main papal office, a room measuring 15 by 40 yards with very high ceilings and three almost full-height windows. In the middle of the room was a kind of board table with twelve chairs around the sides and a papal chair at one end. Here too a variety of religious art tastefully highlighted the room.

At the appointed hour all thirty-six of us—about eighteen priests and the rest laypeople—walked into the papal chapel. In his white robe, Pope John Paul II was kneeling in prayer on a prie-dieu facing the altar and a large metal crucifix and small Marian icon. When we took our seats in four rows facing the front, I was moved to the end of my row because I was tallest and the people behind me wanted to be able to see. The main part of the party was a group from Glasgow, Scotland, and their presence meant that all the hymns and the liturgical readings were in

English, while the Pope celebrated in Latin.

Two priests assisted the Pope along with his personal secretary, who handled the logistics with us visitors calmly, professionally, and in friendly fashion. When Mass began they helped the Holy Father vest, and we sang the opening hymn. The altar faced the wall, so the Holy Father was not facing us directly except when he turned for some of the greetings. Scottish priests read the Epistle and the Gospel. There was no homily; instead, we sat in silence for several minutes, as we did after Communion and again after Mass. For Communion we did not leave our places—the secretary and one of the assistants brought us the Host and the Cup. It was a very prayerful and reverent atmosphere.

When Mass and Thanksgiving were completed we marched out, leaving the Holy Father in the chapel. After divesting, we stood in single file around the perimeter of the papal office, and Pope John Paul soon joined us. He went from person to person and group to group, saying a few words, pausing for a picture, giving a gift of a rosary. When he got to us, the secretary told him we were from Notre Dame. He nodded and said, "Chicago." Not wanting to correct him, we figured that was close enough. We told him we were Holy Cross priests, and he mentioned Cardinal Edward Cassidy who had received an honorary degree last year and had helped provide this opportunity for us.

We clapped when the Pope entered and left the room. I thought he looked healthy but old and infirm. He was shaking a little and there was a noticeable shuffle from his bad hip operation. His head leaned somewhat to the right side. Yet his complexion was hearty and his voice was strong. I had no idea what the rest of his day would entail. He oversees the largest church in the world, with all the challenges that implies. If asked, I would have plenty of advice to offer about various Church policies and priorities, but I must admit that the responsibility he carries is daunting, and all he can do is serve God according to his conscience and his best sense of things.

TAIWANESE PREMIER LIEN CHAN AND PRESIDENT LEE TENG-HUI

During a visit to Taipei in the mid-1990s, I enjoyed a visit with the head of state, Premier Lien Chan, at the equivalent of the White House. The formal meeting room was set up Chinese-style, with chairs arranged in a sweeping oval facing the middle. Between each chair was a small table for ceremonial tea. Three or four photographers and two or three television cameras were on hand, along with the premier's staff. Protocol and hierarchy are important in these situations.

I was seated to the right of the premier, the presumption being that he and I would do most of the talking. Surprisingly, he did not use a translator, although in most diplomatic exchanges a translator is used as a buffer to prevent anything untoward being said. But his English was fine; he had earned a Ph.D. in economics at the University of Chicago.

He spoke of the importance of education and law

enforcement but also stressed the need for additional rehabilitation programs. He articulated a theme that I had also heard in Singapore: "Education is the most important resource for nations that are resource-poor and relatively small in size." The research infrastructure in Taiwanese universities is quite good, especially compared with China. Sports exchanges with the mainland are one way of fostering cooperation. Taiwan is eager to promote the study of Chinese language and culture in other parts of the world, including the United States.

The relationship with mainland China was still sensitive. On the one hand, Taiwan was providing a lot of the capital, funneled through Hong Kong, for economic development in China (and, I might add, reaping good benefits in return); on the other hand, there were no formal interactions or direct air travel between the two, and it was still the policy of the People's Republic of China that Taiwan is a rebellious province.

On another visit, in 1997, I met with Lee Teng-Hui, the first popularly elected president in Taiwan's history. He was seventy-two years old and looked quite healthy, with a warm and engaging smile. He had studied at both Iowa State and Cornell, and his expertise was in agricultural policy. We were greeted at the entrance of the presidential palace by military guards and several presidential aides. The palace has broad open spaces inside, with red carpeting and ceremonial staircases. Upstairs, we were ushered into a meeting room with chairs arranged in the traditional U-shape, which is intended to put the two chief speakers next to each other and spread out the other participants in descending hierarchical order.

The president arrived with his entourage right on time and was announced as "the President of the Republic of China." About ten video and regular cameramen took pictures of the group and then left. President Lee and I did most of the talking, as is customary. At one point he volunteered that he is a Christian and would be giving public witness in some setting soon. He emphasized many times the importance of political freedom and the role that Taiwan could play as a model for all of Asia.

CARDINAL JAIME SIN, THE PHILIPPINES

During a visit to the Philippines in 1994, Bill Beauchamp, Bill Sexton, and I had breakfast at the residence of Cardinal Jaime Sin, who had been very involved politically at the time of the peaceful overthrow of the Marcoses. We all found him to be one of the most fascinating people we had ever met.

Cardinal Sin welcomed us to his home for breakfast and told us a number of dramatic stories. One concerned his role as the first cardinal to visit Gorbachev's Russia. After meeting with the Orthodox Patriarch and visiting a number of churches, he found out later that Gorbachev and Pope John Paul II had been exchanging letters clandestinely before his visit.

A second story picked up on the parallels between the Irish and the Filipinos, both of whom saw many countrymen leave their native lands to disperse around the world, taking their religious heritage and practices with them. During a trip to Italy, the cardinal told us, he was surprised when the CEO of Fiat and his wife wanted to meet with him, and then he discovered that it was because the Filipino housekeeper they employed had brought their whole family back to Catholic religious practice. Later, the Fiat executive made a donation sufficient to subsidize a group of Filipino visitors to Rome for an international assembly at the Vatican.

Cardinal Sin's best-known role was as facilitator of the peaceful mass movement that overthrew the Marcos regime. It began with a request from a group of several hundred military officers to gain protection during a rebellion against the dictator. After consultation with the other bishops in the country, Sin went on the radio to endorse the rebellion, and one million people responded. Eventually, the American government got involved and the Marcoses were flown to Hawaii. At the time of those dramatic events, some Vatican bureaucrats kept sending orders to the bishops not to issue a pastoral letter, so Sin was drafted to fly to Rome where he met with the Pope and found that the bishops had the Pontiff's full support and that he knew nothing about the memos. It emerged that the Vatican delegate to the Philippines was very pro-Marcos and was responsible for the instructions. He was soon replaced.

Jaime Sin was the fourteenth of sixteen children born of a Chinese father and Filipino mother. He was ordained at age twenty-six, made a monsignor at age thirty-one, was a bishop at thirty-eight and an archbishop at forty-four, and became the youngest cardinal at forty-eight. He always had a strong devotion to Mary, and he prays the rosary every day. He had talent as an actor and was known as a witty and practical raconteur.

In his sixties at the time of our visit, Cardinal Sin was friendly, funny, and down-to-earth. When he laughed heartily, he covered his mouth with his hand. His anomalous name for a religious figure was always a source of humor for him. Although he didn't do it with us, he often greeted visitors to his home with the phrase, "Welcome to the House of Sin." It is said that when President Marcos was presented with a plan to assassinate him, the cardinal quipped that assassination would prove he was a mortal Sin.

Cardinal Sin spoke to us affectionately about Notre Dame, where he had received an honorary degree at the time of Ted Hesburgh's retirement. He was quite positive about the religiosity of his country and did not believe that Protestant fundamentalist groups were very successful, despite a heavy investment of money and personnel.

This man was an integral part of profound changes in his country. It was an honor and a privilege to spend so much concentrated, personal time with him.

CARDINAL KIM SOU-HWAN, KOREA

When I visited Cardinal Kim Sou-hwan in 1994, he was the most significant figure in the Korean Catholic Church. In the annual list of the most admired Koreans of whatever background or profession, he was always first—and this in a country where Catholics were 7 percent of the population and Christians about 14 percent. In the era of the military dictatorships, he was one of the few people to speak out, and he did so with wisdom and a sense of proportion. In 1976, Notre Dame awarded him an honorary degree.

When I spoke with Cardinal Kim in his office, his English was very good, even though he had never studied the language formally. Describing the situation of the Church in Korea, he said there were tens of thousands of converts every year in Seoul, and that the same was true with various Protestant groups. Many of the parishes were large, with up to ten thousand parishioners. He had ordained thirty-five priests for the archdiocese the year before, and he expected an equal number that year. The Church, he said, is primarily Korean led and staffed.

Koreans seem much more open to religion as a personal life commitment than the Japanese. The Church in Korea has had thousands of martyrs during periods of persecution. Like the Irish and the Filipinos, Korean Catholics continue to practice their religion when they migrate to other countries.

ARCHBISHOP PHAM MINH MAN AND CARDINAL PHAM DINH TUNG, VIETNAM

During a trip to Saigon in 2002, I paid a visit to Archbishop Pham Minh Man. He seemed to be in his late fifties and was dressed in slacks and a sports shirt. He attended Loyola Marymount University more than thirty years ago, so his English was good. The Catholic Church, he told us, was very much persecuted after the Vietnam War ended. Schools and hospitals were confiscated, and priests, sisters, brothers, and bishops, as well as many laypeople, went to prison or fled the country.

The archbishop described the current situation as improved but far from ideal. For example, the government determines how many seminarians can be accepted every two years, and how many priests can be ordained in each diocese. Financial support comes from Vietnamese Catholics and from Church agencies outside the country. Only recently have the bishops been able to send priests to France, Italy, and the United States for theological education so that they can teach in the seminaries; there are now five hundred Vietnamese priests in the United States.

The churches are full of worshipers, the archbishop told us, and there is no restriction on the number of Masses. Catholics are present in all fields of work, but as non-Communists and non-Party members they cannot rise to the top echelon of leadership. (The Archbishop of Havana, Cuba, told me the same thing.) But it appears that the faith of the people has survived persecution and emigration.

During the same trip to Vietnam, I met with Cardinal Pham Dinh Tung, Archbishop of Hanoi, and his assistant, Father Dang Duc Ngan. The cardinal was eighty-three and somewhat frail, and his coadjutor was eighty-four. Both are still serving because the government refuses to approve their replacements. The archbishop wore a black cassock with red piping and a red beanie. His greeting room was nice enough, but the building itself was in need of repair.

Persecution of the Church was harsher in the North than in the South, and while there has been some easing of government pressure, the cardinal said, the biggest problem Church leadership has is the ability to freely recruit seminarians and gain permission to ordain priests and bishops. This era is less one of concentration camps and more a time of harassment and government refusals to grant permission for the ordination of priests and their assignments by their bishops. To be in charge of the Church in Hanoi is a challenge indeed, because the Communist influence has been so pervasive for so long.

VIOLETA BARRIOS DE CHAMORRO, NICARAGUA

I visited Violeta Barrios de Chamorro, president of Nicaragua from 1990 to 1997, in her home country on two occasions. Following the 1978 assassination of her husband, newspaper publisher Pedro Joaquin Chamorro, Mrs. Chamorro entered politics and led efforts to end the human rights violations of the Somoza regime. She upset the incumbent president, Daniel Ortega of the revolutionary Sandinista Party, and during her term helped put an end to the decade-long Contra war as well as working to reform the military and improve the economy. Our first meeting was in the winter of 2000, a few months before Notre Dame awarded her an honorary degree. By then she was serving as president of a foundation named for her that is dedicated to the preservation of peace and democracy in Nicaragua.

We met in her modest but lovely home, which had a typical patio garden in the middle. Our conversation took place in her husband's former office, which was full of memorabilia. He not only spent time in prison but was under constant death threats for his paper's criticism of the Somoza regime, and he was eventually murdered by Somoza's soldiers. Mrs. Chamorro read from letters he had sent to the family from prison, including one addressed to her and the children just before he was killed. The import of that final message was how he hated to put his family at risk, but that he felt a Christian moral obligation to speak the truth about the realities of Nicaragua. It was a moving and impressive visit.

Three years later, when I paid another visit to Mrs. Chamorro's home, she gave me the great privilege of a tour of her office, which contains all the gifts, honorary degrees, tokens of appreciation, and honors that she received during her years as president and since. She is a woman of deep faith who has effectively become the mother and the conscience of Nicaragua.

CARDINAL OSCAR RODRIGUEZ, HONDURAS

During a visit to Honduras in 2003, I presented the Notre Dame–Coca-Cola Award for Distinguished Public Service in Latin America to Cardinal Oscar Rodriguez. The award consists of two checks worth $10,000 each—one for the honoree and one for a designated charity. Cardinal Rodriguez is an old friend who has been to our campus a number of times. Fluent in seven languages, he was the head of CELAM (the Bishops' Conference of Latin America) and is now a major spokesperson internationally for debt relief. He also has developed one of the best lay missionary programs in Latin America. During lunch we had a wide-ranging discussion about Honduras, about the Church in Latin America, and about the Pope and the Vatican at that particular moment of Church history. Having met a cross-section of cardinals who might realistically be considered for the next Pope, I favor Cardinal Rodriguez.

CARDINAL PIO LAGHI, THE VATICAN

During a visit to Rome in the summer of 1995, I had an opportunity to meet Cardinal Pio Laghi, Prefect of the Vatican's Congregation on Education. He is Italian by birth but has spent a career as a Vatican diplomat, including a stint in the United States as head of the Vatican's U.S. delegation. While in this country he became a football fan and would come to our campus annually to watch a game. About a year before our Rome meeting, he spent four days at Notre Dame for the worldwide assembly of the International Federation of Catholic Universities.

Cardinal Laghi's English is excellent, and he knows the American scene better than most bureaucrats in the Curia. We spoke for about an hour in a friendly and straightforward fashion. I described the ongoing work of the *Ex Corde Ecclesiae* Committee in the United States, in which he was very interested. He seemed content to let the process work itself out without rushing things. We also discussed Catholic education around the world, drawing on people we met and things we learned on previous trips abroad. Tim Scully, who was with me for the meeting, described the Alliance for Catholic Education (ACE) program that he initiated, which sends recent Notre Dame graduates, after summer training, to teach in Catholic grade schools and high schools. After two years in the classroom, plus two summers at Notre Dame taking education courses, the students receive a master's degree in education. The cardinal saw this as an excellent example of the American commitment to Catholic education, this time staffed by laypeople.

We also puzzled together about the most effective strategy for reviving Catholic education in Africa.

CARDINAL ROGER ETCHEGARAY, THE VATICAN

During a Rome visit in the mid-1990s, I paid a visit to the home of Cardinal Roger Etchegaray, president of the Pontifical Council for Justice and Peace and a Notre Dame honorary degree recipient in 1994 who made a great hit with everyone on our campus. The cardinal had become the chief troubleshooter for Pope John Paul II and had visited Lebanon, Somalia, Croatia, Haiti, and China, among other places. We discussed all those places during the course of the dinner. We also talked about the United Nations and the American attitude toward that body; the Council for Justice and Peace is heavily involved with various U.N. agencies.

The cardinal is sociable, warm, and hospitable, with a big smile and a gracious manner. He is a French Basque with a solid, muscular body and deep inner strength. He reminds me of the Pope, with whom he seems to have a close relationship. His English is limited, so we were joined by one of his staff, Sister Marjorie Keenan, R.S.H.M., an American nun who accompanied him on his trip to Notre Dame. We had a simple but tasty meal, with wine and champagne in honor of Sister Marjorie, who was celebrating her birthday. The cardinal had just recovered from prostate surgery but seemed to be feeling much better.

I enjoyed spending time with him to build on the relationship established during his visit to Notre Dame.

CARDINAL AGOSTINO CASAROLI, THE VATICAN

In the summer of 1995, I had a meeting with Cardinal Agostino Casaroli, former Vatican Secretary of State, in his suite of apartments behind St. Peter's. (Then age eighty, he died in 1998.) We talked for about forty-five minutes, and his manner was warm and gracious. He was dressed in a black cassock with red sash and beanie. In a glass cabinet was a gift inscribed from Kurt Waldheim, the former president of Austria. The cardinal recalled a past visit to Notre Dame and regretted that he had not been able to accept our offer of an honorary degree in 1989.

He is best remembered for his work relating to Central and Eastern Europe and the U.S.S.R. With a Polish Pope, as with Pope Paul VI before him, the outreach to the East was a high priority. I suspect that none of them imagined the profound changes that would take place in their lifetime. He mentioned in passing that Paul VI had discouraged him from keeping a diary, but he said he was now spending time trying to reconstruct the events of that exciting period of Vatican diplomacy. He was also involved in the last stages of a border dispute between Chile and Argentina, and he said that Ecuador had recently sought mediation from Rome in its brief war with Peru, but Peru was not amenable.

Throughout his time in Rome he had a ministry to inmates in juvenile detention facilities, which seemed to give him great joy. The inmates did not have a clue what a cardinal was.

AUDREY DONNITHORNE, CHINA

When I was in Hong Kong in the winter of 1996, my traveling companions and I went to the apartment of an extraordinary lady for Mass and conversation. Audrey Donnithorne was born of Anglican missionary parents in China's Sichuan Province. In her late teens she returned to China for three years and then earned a bachelor's degree at Oxford. She converted to Catholicism at the age of twenty-one, having decided that the Church is not only a spiritual entity but one that needs to be incarnated in the world as a corporate entity. She taught at London University and at Australian National University, and in 1967 published a book titled *China's Economic System*, which is still regarded as a major study.

In 1980 Audrey began visiting China to lecture; while there, she also was in touch with Church leaders. In 1985 she set up a private company to produce Chinese-language books for the Chinese Catholic Church that were given away. By the time of my visit, fifty volumes of theology, Scripture, and catechetics had been published in press runs of 3,000 to 5,000. Since her retirement not long before our visit, Audrey had been serving the needs of the Catholic Church in China. She told us she believed that the Church in China is vibrant in many places, that it is increasing rapidly in size, and that there is great demand for priests to go on sick calls. China, she said, has a spiritual vacuum, and some feel that if the Communist Party vanished, there would be chaos.

Audrey was living in simple digs. She had a large personal library, and copies of her volumes intended for the Church in China. We were all impressed by her simplicity, her holiness, and the importance of her postretirement work.

BISHOP ALOYSIUS JIN LUXIAN, SHANGHAI

During a stop in Shanghai in the winter of 1996, I visited a convent and novitiate for religious women under Bishop

Aloysius Jin Luxian. I celebrated Mass in English for a congregation of about 150 sisters, plus Bishop Jin, and afterward I had a simple breakfast with the bishop.

What Bishop Jin did in Shanghai was recreate the Catholic Church and modernize it. The life and practices of China's "aboveground" Church—called the "Patriotic Church" because it is approved by the government—are in line with Vatican II, and priests and sisters enjoy opportunities to study abroad and bring back what they learn. The Church in Shanghai has also been a catalyst for other parts of China. The bishop called himself a "happy beggar," since most of what he has achieved has been supported financially by Catholics elsewhere.

All that is missing is reconciliation with the underground church and formal union with Rome. I hope and pray that day will come soon.

HUGO BANZER, BOLIVIA

During a visit to Bolivia early in 2001, I met with President Hugo Banzer, who was much criticized in certain circles for his policies and friends during his first eight years in office. Sorting out the evidence is difficult, however, because that was a time of heavy ideological conflict between Soviet and U.S. spheres of influence in Latin America, and CIA money was pouring into regions that were overtly anti-Communist. The president, who was short and thin and far from the image of a military leader and three-time head of state, welcomed us graciously into his home. He told me his parents were poor and had sent him off to a Catholic school because there were few educational options in his part of Bolivia. Eventually he was accepted into a military academy and graduated as a lieutenant in the army. Later he went to Fort Knox for tank training and also spent time at the Bolivian Embassy in Washington, D.C. In retrospect, he said, both his military service and his government service came out of a common sense of vocation.

President Banzer told me he and his wife are very Catholic, with a strong devotion to the Virgin Mary, and the most common paintings and statues in his residence were Marian images given to him as gifts. Of his five children, three girls and two boys, both sons were dead—one murdered, purportedly for political reasons, the other killed in the States in a motorcycle accident.

He spoke of his commitment to the eradication of coca farming, which is the base crop in the production of cocaine for the world market. He also referred to the problem of poverty, the need for economic development, and the importance of education. At one point he said that he really didn't enjoy the presidency, because there were so many problems to deal with. The previous year, for example, had seen confrontations between rural farmers and the government, and food shipments to La Paz were cut off for three weeks. A state of emergency was declared and a number of people were killed or injured. While Bolivia has no history of guerrilla activity or organized kidnapping, some indigenous power groups have that potential.

Throughout our conversation, President Banzer was

soft-spoken and engaging. Toward the end of the visit, Mrs. Banzer came in for a few moments. At a certain point, I asked who won when the president and his wife disagreed. He quickly offered that she did, since she is from Cochabamba and such people are always the smartest in Bolivia, especially when they no longer live in Cochabamba.

President Banzer struck me as a man who has changed over time and now finds himself in the twilight of his political career. Whatever he may have done in his younger days, he seemed genuinely committed to the well-being of the nation within a democratic framework.

CARDINAL CAHAL DALY, IRELAND

Several times in the 1990s I visited Cardinal Cahal Daly, the Primate of Ireland, in Armagh. Before he became a bishop he was a professor of scholastic philosophy for more than twenty years at Queen's University, Belfast. He was invited to receive an honorary degree at our commencement in 1991 but had to cancel at the last minute— it seemed connected to the Irish archbishop who was discovered to have fathered a child. We made a second offer in 1993, and he was able to come then and accept an honorary doctor of laws degree.

One Irish-American group wrote us letters protesting the honorary degree invitation because they considered the cardinal too condemnatory of the IRA and insufficiently supportive of the MacBride Principles (fair-employment, affirmative-action principles put forward as a corporate code of conduct for U.S. companies doing business in Northern Ireland). But he was highly regarded by his priests and was considered by the Protestants and the British to be a voice for moderation.

Each time we met I found myself really taken with the man. He was thoughtful, undefensive, engaging, and very clear and logical in his analysis of issues, yet he had a gentle manner and a lively wit.

AFTERWORD

In the first-year undergraduate seminar that I have been teaching since I became president, I summarize the goal of the course as employing novels and films to understand human persons and social groups from a variety of historical and cultural settings. Our aim is to seek insight and understanding in a world undergoing rapid change and troubled by conflict and hostility. In such a course, I am trying to provide a format in which my students can travel vicariously and through the mode of verbal and visual stories to try to engage with a greater degree of understanding and sympathy the experience and circumstances of people different from themselves.

In the journal sections and snapshots of this book, I am sharing a bit of what I have learned along the way. In the rich variety of people and circumstances that I have experienced firsthand, I have come to appreciate the great beauty of God's creation and the wide range of social, economic, and political circumstances in which the world's people live. I have always returned home stimulated, enriched, and desirous of learning more.

I have found that one trip builds upon another, that one set of challenges gives me the courage and desire to explore anew the unknown and the unfamiliar. I have traveled at a time in history when oceans can be quickly crossed, and even in the direst of circumstances one can easily find reasonable accommodations and persons proficient in the local language.

In the end, I guess the reader learns as much about the traveler as about destinations visited. I am happy to share these special moments and prized people with you, if only vicariously. I thank you for accompanying me along the way.